Essentials of Healthcare Strategy and Performance Management

Leaders of healthcare organizations, and students aspiring to become one, should be asking themselves one thing in these financially challenging times: how can we maintain a strategic and competitive advantage over other players in their market? Some healthcare organizations have faced extremely poor financial performance in recent years, with data suggesting that up to 10% of hospitals will go bankrupt or face closure within the next 10 years. Yet, little pragmatic evidence exists to offer insights into how to create better strategies to improve performance, build resiliency, and align stakeholders.

Essentials of Healthcare Strategy and Performance Management explores the most critical components of business strategy and performance management for modern, complex healthcare organizations. Using pragmatic and real-world evidence, this book provides essential briefings on key topics that every current or aspiring leader needs to know in order to better manage strategy and achieve improved performance in their hospital or health system. We will also specifically focus on implementation of strategy, and best practices for some of the most important quality management techniques. We hope this book helps inspire leaders to be creative in formulating more effective competitive strategy.

Essentials of Healthcare Strategy and Performance Management

A Practical Guide for Executives and Emerging Leaders

James R. Langabeer, PhD
Tiffany Champagne-Langabeer, PhD

Routledge
Taylor & Francis Group

A PRODUCTIVITY PRESS BOOK

First published 2024
by Routledge
605 Third Avenue, New York, NY 10158

and by Routledge
4 Park Square, Milton Park, Abingdon, Oxon, OX14 4RN

Routledge is an imprint of the Taylor & Francis Group, an informa business

ISBN: 978-1-032-62371-9 (hbk)
ISBN: 978-1-032-62370-2 (pbk)
ISBN: 978-1-032-62372-6 (ebk)

DOI: 10.4324/9781032623726

Typeset in Garamond
by codeMantra

Dedication

This book is dedicated to all our healthcare clients that we have worked with and learned so much from. We also appreciate our former graduate students who have helped to improve the quality of the material as it's been taught in our strategy and leadership classes over the last decade. Lastly, this is dedicated to all those aspiring and current healthcare executives who are drivers of change in the industry. We hope this book challenges you all to dream big and love to lead.

Contents

An Invitation for Strategic Thinking

Here is the main emphasis of all that follows in this book: healthcare executives need to start thinking more strategically to embrace the changes and potential disruptive innovations that could derail many organizations. Technology such as artificial intelligence or blockchain, gene editing and genomic engineering, and broad use of mobile applications for healthcare are all going to change the dynamics of healthcare organizations considerably. Healthcare executives must be prepared to strategically lead these changes. We can't even predict what or where the changes will really come from, but we must try and be ready for it. Strategy matters, and better performance is the ultimate holy grail. Executives must learn how to get involved in strategy, as well as when to involve their board, and when to step out of the way.

As executives, get ready to embrace strategic thinking. Leaders, both those emerging and those who are established, don't have time to read a lengthy textbook to learn about the latest strategy techniques. *Essentials of Healthcare Strategy and Performance Management* explores only the most critical components of business strategy and performance management for modern healthcare organizations, and we try to cover these topics in a relatively brief and concise manner. Using pragmatic and real-world evidence, this book will provide essential briefings on key topics that every current or aspiring leader needs to know to better manage strategy and achieve improved performance in their company, clinic, hospital, or health system.

Why does strategy matter? Because your organization is counting on you to be sustainable, to earn a profit or at least break even, and to set direction for years to come. Strategy is not a written document, and it's not a static object.

It's a real, dynamic game plan for where you are headed and how you intend to get there. Managing performance requires you to identify what is working well, and adapting where necessary to maintain high levels of performance.

Drawing on emerging best practices, this book offers actionable guidance on how to make strategy more effective in your hospital, retail pharmacy, laboratory, health department, health insurance corporation, or any other healthcare organization. We hope you enjoy.

Acknowledgments

If you are reading this, you are probably interested in creating more effective strategies, leading complex organizations, and innovating within healthcare. Some of you may be new to the industry, while others have been around a long time. Either way, this book is designed to give you insights to improve the strategic decisions in your healthcare organization. I have found that busy executives would much rather be concise and efficient with their time—the most important resource we have. I have been fortunate to consult with many bright forward-thinking healthcare clients that have helped me to better understand the unique aspects of the industry. Many of these were also my PhD students, who have gone on to very senior roles throughout the country There are so many executives who are highly skilled and intelligent and have helped me to form some of these thoughts in this book, and for all of you—thank you!

Several excellent professors and practitioners have contributed to this book, and you will see a few chapters written by those authors. I appreciate their assistance greatly to help make this book stronger and more relevant.

–James

Author and Contributors List

James R. Langabeer, PhD, MBA, FACHE
University of Texas Health Science
  Center at Houston

Tiffany Champagne-Langabeer, PhD, RDN, FHIMSS
University of Texas Health Science
  Center at Houston

Jeff Helton, PhD, FHFMA, CMA, CFE
University of Colorado Denver
  Business School

Karima Lalani, PhD, FACHE
University of Washington School of
  Public Health

With Contributions by

Erin Donnelly, MHA
University of Colorado Denver
  Business School

About the Authors

James R. Langabeer, PhD, MBA, FACHE, is the Robert Graham Professor of Entrepreneurial Informatics and Director of the Center for Behavioral Emergency and Addiction Research at the University of Texas Health Science Center at Houston. He is also an independent healthcare strategy consultant, and founder of Yellowstone Advisors, which advises leaders on strategy and operational improvement. He has served in senior leadership at several academic medical centers, including deputy controller and head of supply chain at M.D. Anderson Cancer Center. He has taught strategy, decision-making, and finance at both Boston University and the University of Texas. During his career, he also served as the founding CEO of a leading health information exchange organization and was the COO for a successful business intelligence company that was later sold to a Fortune 100 firm. James holds a PhD in Management Sciences from the University of Lancaster in England, an MBA from Baylor University, and a BBA from the University of Texas at San Antonio. He is a Fellow of both the American College of Healthcare Executives and the Healthcare Information and Management Systems Society, and holds the Certified Management Accountant and Certified Fraud Examiner designations.

Tiffany Champagne-Langabeer, PhD, RDN, FHIMSS, is an Associate Professor of Biomedical Informatics and Public Health at the University of Texas Health Science Center at Houston. Her previous work and educational training have focused on the transformation of healthcare through collaboration and joint venture by managing processes, modifying behaviors, and collecting data for outcomes research. She served as the Vice President for the Greater Houston Health Healthconnect, the health information exchange organization covering most of the state. She has taught management and leadership courses over the past 20 years and earned her PhD in Public Health, focused on management and policy sciences. She has an undergraduate degree in Nutrition from the University of Texas at Austin and is a licensed and registered dietitian (RDN), as well as a Fellow of the Healthcare Information and Management Systems Society.

Contributing Authors

Erin Donnelly, MHA, is an Adjunct Professor in the University of Colorado Denver Healthcare Administration MBA Program. She is also currently the Director of Strategic Planning at the Children's Hospital of Colorado. She has served as the Vice President of Strategy for Centura Health, an integrated delivery system located in Colorado and Western Kansas. She was also the Chief Strategy Officer at Intermountain Primary Children's Hospital in Salt Lake City, Utah. Erin currently teaches both healthcare strategic management and healthcare leadership courses at the University of Colorado Denver. Additionally, Erin serves as a coach for graduate student teams at national health administration case competitions. Erin holds a Master of Healthcare Administration from the University of Minnesota and a Bachelor of Science in Biology from Boston College.

Jeff Helton, PhD, FHMA, CMA, CFE, is a Professor and Director of the health administration program at the University of Colorado Denver Business School. He is considered an expert in healthcare financial operations management, healthcare process analysis and benchmarking, health information technology, and healthcare fraud detection, with many industry publications. He holds a Master's degree in Hospital and Health Administration from the University of Alabama at Birmingham and a PhD in Healthcare Policy and Management from the University of Texas School of Public Health. He holds the Certified Management Accountant and Certified Fraud Examiner designations, and is a Fellow of the Healthcare Financial Management Association.

Karima Lalani, PhD, MBA, FACHE, is an Assistant Teaching Professor and Director of Health Informatics and Health Information Management degree programs at the University of Washington School of Public Health in Seattle. Dr. Lalani is a seasoned healthcare management and informatics researcher and professional, with over 15 years of experience in healthcare workforce education and training, strategic planning, healthcare finance, and digital health, and continues to publish in these areas. Dr. Lalani participates on the editorial review panel for the journal *BMJ Health & Care Informatics* and continues to present at state, national, and international conferences. She holds a PhD in Health Policy and Management from the University of Texas School of Public Health and is a Registered Health Information Administrator (RHIA) and a Fellow of the American College of Healthcare Executive.

STRATEGIC THINKING

1

Chapter 1

Strategy and Competition

The Need for Strategic Thinking

More than any other time, the healthcare industry today offers both enormous opportunities and significant challenges. Recent shifts in consumer attitudes toward wellness, improved nutrition, reversing the aging process, and better understanding of behavioral and mental health are opening doors for new devices, supplements, and services like never before. Innovation, through artificial intelligence, is helping to improve early detection and diagnoses, and improve the care delivery process. Yet difficult challenges remain for the chief and senior executives, such as changing reimbursement mechanisms, complex layers of legislation, and competition from multiple segments of the industry.

Nothing predicts the performance of a company better than the strength of their leadership team. In healthcare, this is true more than ever. Leaders that are good only in one area, such as accounting or provider relations, will not make it. We must be aware of strategy, competitors, markets, technological innovations, and other new opportunities.

Defining Strategy

Many organizational theorists have tried to capture the essence of strategy. Michael Porter famously proposed that strategy is about competitive positioning, or how you decide to position your organization's offerings within the marketplace (Porter, 1996). Henry Mintzberg, another famous strategist,

DOI: 10.4324/9781032623726-2

in 1987 summarized the major theories about strategy as being in one of five areas: strategy could represent position, plans, patterns, ploy, or perspective. Each of these is a good representation of what strategy can be.

But here, let's start with a general definition of **strategy**: my favorite definition is that strategy is the pattern of high-impact choices that determine the strategic direction for an organization. Strategy involves responding to matters that are long-term, future-oriented, high-value, and significant (Whittington et al., 2023). So in this book, when we talk about strategic decisions and management, we're referring to the small subset of activities undertaken by leaders that are focused on the big picture for the future, are often associated with significant amount of resources, and are important to the direction of the organization. Separating these big issues from the less-important ones is necessary, since busy executives need to prioritize and place greater effort into those areas that matter most.

When most managers think about the term strategy, they think about bound documents holding strategic plans and somewhat mundane annual exercises. And for many organizations, that is true. Their only real involvement in strategy is doing an annual update. Effective healthcare leaders should try to re-shape this internally, because strategy is much more than that—strategy is the basis for competing, and succeeding, in a crowded healthcare market.

Strategy, specifically an organizational (or corporate) strategy, is what creates high-performing organizations and separates them from the distressed ones. This is the top level of strategy within an organization, which helps determine the overall positioning and how value is created internally by all of the sub-units, divisions, and affiliated businesses. Strategy here though is not just laying out a purpose and a vision, it has to be acted upon by the various units.

In our own research, we found that 15% of all acute hospitals for instance are financially distressed and could be out of business in the next few years (Langabeer et al., 2018). Leaders want to avoid that kind of position. Solid strategy enables leaders to achieve their vision and goals. Strategy is what makes healthcare leader CVS Pharmacy acquire six companies in the 5 years leading up to 2023, including Aetna for a whopping $77 billion USD (Berryman, 2023). Strategy is what makes great hospitals, like M.D. Anderson Cancer Center, create and fulfill big visions, such as "Making Cancer History ®". Strategy is the basis for how to compete and win.

Although strategy matters most to the top of the organization, it affects everyone internally as the strategic direction has to be implemented and enabled by the lower-level officers and managers. People outside the organization are key stakeholders and partners as well, including bond analysts, investors, banks, patients, vendors, the media, and communities.

There are many sectors within the healthcare industry. These include retail pharmacy stores, long-term care facilities, acute care hospitals, ambulatory surgery centers, outpatient facilities, medical device manufacturers, health payers or insurance firms, medical device manufacturers, medical supply firms, distributors, health technology companies, and specialty pharmaceuticals manufacturers, to name a few. Some sectors are inherently more financially profitable than others (such as pharmaceuticals), while other companies barely break a profit (such as hospitals). What ties all these diverse firms together is that ultimately, they all aim to impact the health of populations and individuals, and they share a lot of strategic similarities. Yet financial performance is only one component of organizational health, and we less often focus on metrics involving customers, markets, and employees. How do you improve your organization's performance, especially if you don't measure where you are today and have a vision for where you want to go? We have to start by re-examining strategy and the nature of how we compete for our patients (or clients) and share of the market.

If healthcare organizations are to prosper, they must re-define their own competitive strategy unique to their environment and market.

Case 1.1: Sperio Health

Sperio Health's CEO, Janice Ryman, was concerned about their most recent drop in market valuation, which impacted their debt financing payments. She called together her six chiefs that reported directly for a de-brief. The chief financial officer (CFO) reported that costs had gone up and that they needed to trim back. The marketing head said that no changes in advertising could be made right now, unless it would destroy their branding strategy. The clinical executive talked about how patients were giving 95%+ patient satisfaction scores. Service lines were generally content with what they're doing. What are they missing?

The director of strategy, Tom Smith, took the lead in trying to re-frame some of the biggest investments and decisions made over the last 3 years. Tom talked about how they created an alliance with a medical device company a few years ago but backed out after 1 year because of board-level disagreements. They all nodded their head remembering the deal. The partnership with the medical school was recently put out to bid by procurement in an attempt to save money, despite not having other sources of supply. This caused a lot of tension with their school partner who immediately opened up their own group practices and started looking for new hospital alliances. Tom mentioned the three new site locations created largely to make better use of existing facilities.

As a strategist, when looking at this, what do you see? If strategy is a reflection of the long-term direction and the patterns of choices made, Sperio Health seems to be lacking any consistency. Strategy might be emerging, but it's largely not a result of contemplation, analyses, or well-crafted visions. Sperio Health ultimately was purchased by a private equity firm for half its valuation 2 years later.

Competitive Strategy

One component of overall strategy is **competitive strategy**, focused on how to win over your competition. Competition is one of those words that everybody feels intuitively understands, yet the distinction between competitors and collaborators is largely disappearing and the lines are being blurred, so it's useful to have a more precise definition. **Competition** exists when two or more players in a market attempt to reach or serve the same group of customers, with both trying to gain an advantage over the other to win a share of the market. Competition exists for for-profit companies, non-profit organizations, membership organizations, social service agencies, and all other forms of business. Even in government!

It's important to think about competition in terms of multiple dimensions: location (or geography you choose to focus), market (the products and services a firm offers), and technology (the delivery method for your offerings). Many organizations tend to think of their competitors in very narrow terms, such as those in the same city. This is an inaccurate view. Competitors can come from anywhere, as many providers have found out when online telehealth visits skyrocketed post-COVID and took away many patients and primary care visits. Organizations must differentiate beyond geography, technology, and service type to improve their competitive positioning.

Strategy, as direction, does not occur in a vacuum. It has to be considered alongside the market that it has been established for and the competitors which exist. You might have a great strategy, but in your specific region, it doesn't work. Competition can also mute your strategy. You attempt to build a series of new services, and competitors announce even larger plans for the same.

Good competitors also create better markets for everybody, because typically the best ideas, products, and services at more reasonable costs survive and win. This forces everyone to keep innovating and finding ways to improve.

Competitive strategy therefore at the most basic level is how an organization chooses to compete with others in their market. This requires two things:

1. You have to understand who you are competing with, and
2. You can't compete unless you do something unique or different.

Competitive strategy is comprised of both what you intended to do (your intent or plans) and your actions (the patterns that emerge in your major decisions and policies). Competitive strategy should focus on one major topic—addressing the question of "what advantage does our company have over others?", but should also help identify "who, what, why, where, and when".

A well-conceived strategy will help you select ideal locations, services, and pricing that makes you stand out from competitors. Understanding the competition is really important here—if you don't know how you are—different, better, lower cost, or unique—then, you don't really have a strategy. If you are a senior executive or board member, ask yourself this: what is my organization truly outstanding at? What is it best known for? If you can't think of the answer, or it's not entirely positive, you must focus on re-defining your business strategy. Take steps today to get your senior executives in one room, hire an independent consultant to help provide structure, and focus on the competitive strategy for the coming year (Figure 1.1).

Yet having the best statement of strategy won't get you far if you don't have the internal human or financial resources to pull it off. Your role as a senior executive is to set strategy that will be effective given your internal resources and capabilities or figure out how to bring those into the organization. That's why leadership is so important in determining who wins and who loses. Weisz and Vassolo argue that executives should "treat strategic planning as a leadership intervention" (2022).

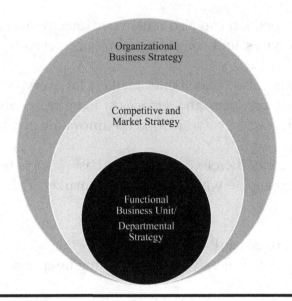

Figure 1.1   Levels of organizational strategy.

A generic business strategy, such as just being the lowest cost provider, or just focusing on operational effectiveness doesn't necessarily work in healthcare (Porter, 1996). It helps of course to be extremely efficient, since many health organizations are not, but that is not necessarily sufficient to create a long-term competitive advantage. You have to think of multiple angles on which you can compete differently. These are examples of some specific strategies that are working for many organizations, all of which we will touch on here in this book.

- Joining or creating strategic alliances of providers in target markets
- Developing a reputation for one or two major service lines
- Developing a brand awareness as the premier provider of a product or service
- Developing a more comprehensive digital strategy for engaging patients
- Creating alliances and partnerships that help to expand services and coverage

There are no simple solutions, and that's why competitive strategy helps you stand out.

Strategy as Practice

Although strategy represents patterns of choices and long-term direction, there are alternative views of strategy that are more practice oriented. Oxford University Saïd Business School defines strategy fundamentally through four Ps: purpose, players, partnerships, and processes (Whittington et al., 2023). Purpose represents the strategic intent that binds the organization together. Purpose is what the organization is there for, who it serves, and why it exists. Purpose is more than just mission or vision, and it's the organization culture and ethos that bind people together. Players are the entire set of stakeholders, not just customers and employees, but regulators, shareholders, government, and communities. Partners refer to your vendors and collaborators, up- and down-stream that help create value for your organization. This is not an operational view of vendors, but one in which strategy is formulated collectively with the players to help your organization compete. In healthcare, this would entail suppliers, distributors, manufacturers, and others. Processes refer to the connections and protocols implemented that help organizations execute and repeat processes with minimal waste and error. Together, these four (purpose, players, partners, and processes) need to be fundamental elements of your strategy.

Case 1.2: Minton Medical Supplies

Minton Medical is a small regional manufacturer of general medical supplies, including surgical gloves, medical cups, and syringe aspirators. Their chief financial officer (CFO) just ran the January month-end close and discovered that inventory losses were double that of previous months. She brought this to the president's attention, warning of potential losses again this month. A strategy review was initiated to see what product lines were selling well, in what regions, and what could be done to improve. A small consultancy was hired to help with the analyses. Strategically, the products made by Minton were all very generic, and competitors were fierce. Large national distributors such as McKesson and Cardinal Health made similar products and owned much of the market share. Minton's success had largely come from a few big medical centers in the Midwest where they had great relations with the head of procurement. The strategic analyses showed that only a handful of the stockkeeping units (SKU) actually earned any margin, and others only sold in certain locations but not in others.

Looking at this information, it became apparent that Minton's strategic purpose was unclear. They did not have a cost-leadership position, and they did not have national brand or market share. Their competitive strategy had worked up to now, but cost pressures are forcing a full re-evaluation. The CFO and the president decided now would be a good time to strategically re-think their intent, building on a few core competencies. They launched "Red Ocean Strategy 2030" and developed a cross-functional team with customer representation to reassess their strategy and objectives.

Results Orientation

If you are a senior leader or the chief executive, you need to be focused on results. Results are the outcomes, and they are more than just financial, although that is often a dominant measure of success. Of course, financial metrics are important, but they're not everything because the results from long-term direction do not always coincide with accounting periods. You must take into account all aspects of performance, which we term organizational health. These core dimensions best represent overall health of an organization: financial performance, strategic direction, agility and learning, growth, and organizational culture. We will spend more time talking about these in the chapter on performance management (Figure 1.2).

Leaders should be looking for how to maintain a competitive advantage over other facilities in my market and answering these questions:

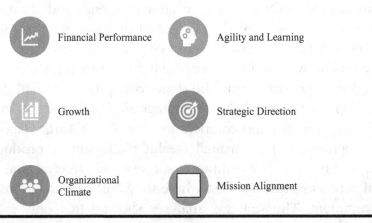

Figure 1.2 **Comprehensive organizational health.**

- What kind of organization (firm, hospital, company) am I trying to create?
- How do I stay profitable, maintain high quality and service levels to customers/patients, and retain and develop your people and providers?
- How can I initiate changes that will influence the long-term direction?

The answers to those questions are the key to growth and long-term survival, and they impact your organization's strategic position, which ultimately is the measure of fit between your intentions and your organizational realities. By realities, we mean the market that you face, the environment you compete in, the level of assets and resources you have to utilize, and the fit internally within your own culture. **Strategic positioning** involves aligning your intended strategy with all of these external and internal factors to ensure success. The result of your strategic positioning is a **competitive advantage**—a condition that causes you to be in a favorable position relative to your competitors.

But how do you get there? This is the age-old question we've been asking for some time. How and why do some companies get extraordinary growth and performance, while others lag behind? These strategic performance indicators (people-financial-quality-service) are what allow organizations to continue to prosper.

These are the specific strengths that are unique to your organization, and really distinguish you from the other competitors. Differentiating from others is key to growth and long-term survival—but, how do you get there? This is the age-old question we've been asking for some time. How and why do some companies get extraordinary growth and performance, while others lag behind?

Strategic Intent

The primary purpose of a senior leader is to influence the strategic positioning and strategic intent of the organization overall. If you are new to an organization, you might feel you have little control over the strategy, but this isn't accurate. Each member of leadership teams can influence the strategy in unique and subtle ways. Navigating your personal growth can help you avoid frustrations when your perspectives are not always adopted or appreciated.

Purpose or intent is not solely your idea of what the organization is about. It is the organization's "why"—why are we in business? What role do we serve? How can we uniquely contribute to this area of healthcare?

Intent needs to be based on a shared vision, with your key partners and players. Shared implies collective and agreed upon. As a senior leader, you obviously need to make your intent known. But that purpose has to be "sold", negotiated, and communicated broadly to get others in alignment and on-board with that vision. Find alignment between your mission, vision, strategic objectives, and initiatives with all of your strategic partners.

If you find yourself in the C-suite, attempt to address two important questions in strategic intent (Di Fiore, 2014):

1. What do you want to offer your target customers, and
2. Why is your organization's value proposition any different from your competitors?

The second question addresses why and how is your firm unique from all other players in the market, community, or industry. Unique and differentiated products and services help create long-term success. Now the hard part—can you capsulate that into a unique strategy statement? An "elevator pitch" or short summary of where you are headed, who you serve, and how you are different? This is the organization's purpose—its reason for existing.

We will focus on leadership's role in strategy in Chapters 6 and 7, but for now, ask yourself this question:

■ How Can I (as a Healthcare Executive) Influence This Intent and Help to Enable It?

Strategy maps, a concept developed by Robert Kaplan from the Harvard Business School, helps to translate the various perspectives on outcomes into specific strategic objectives and initiatives that must be initiated to align the organization. A simple version of the strategy map is shown in Figure 1.3.

Ask a healthcare CEO what their strategy is, and it will be difficult to clearly articulate this in terms that differentiate, or stand apart, from others in the market. According to Collis and Rukstad (2008), very few executives have the ability to succinctly describe their strategy. This lack of ability to communicate directly and clearly where you intend to go, and how this makes you unique, often results in an inability for the organization to move together in a coordinated way.

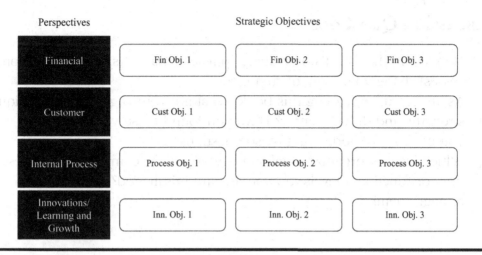

Figure 1.3 Strategy map.

If you are a new C-level employee, your first task must be to collaboratively create and express this strategy, so others can follow. Leaders can't lead without clear and consistent direction.

Remember that intent can be both explicit, or expressed (e.g., what leaders say publicly or on their website, interviews, or reports), and implicit, which results from the underlying meaning behind the choices that are made. Each time a strategic decision is made, strategic intent is modified.

Chapter Summary

- Think of strategy as direction and patterns of choices that can be influenced through leadership.
- Leaders need to examine both their explicit strategic intent and the intent that is conveyed unintentionally through choices.
- Competitors can come from anywhere, beyond your geographic market, and need to be examined very broadly.
- To get started, focus on what you are trying to offer your target customers, and how you are differentiated in your value proposition.

Discussion Questions

1. How could the four Ps of strategy (purpose, partners, players, and processes) shape your view of strategy?
2. As an executive reading this book, what are your organization's unique strengths and differentiators? Have you found these yet? What tools will you use to start addressing these questions?
3. Which level of organizational strategy (top level, competitive business unit, or functional levels) do you feel are misaligned? How can you re-align them?

Key Terms

Competition; Competitive Advantage; Competitive Strategy; Strategic Positioning; Strategy

References

Berryman L (2023). Signify Health Chats Acquisition by CVS Health. June 19, 2023. Available at https://www.modernhealthcare.com/mergers-ac-oak-street

Collis DJ and Rukstad MG (2008). Can you say what your strategy is? *Harvard Business Review*, 84, 1–10.

DiFiore A (2014). The art of crafting a 15-word strategy statement. *Harvard Business Review*, Feb 12, 2014, reprint H0009E.

Langabeer J, Lalani K, Champagne-Langabeer T, and Helton J (2018). Predicting financial distress in acute care hospitals. *Hospital Topics*, 96(3), 75–79.

Mintzberg, H (1987). The strategy concept: five Ps for strategy. *California Management Review*, 30(1), 11–24.

Porter M (1996). What is strategy? For starters, it's not the same as operational effectiveness. *Harvard Business Review*, 96608, 1–20.

Weisz N and Vassolo R. (2022). What you lose with your new strategy. *Harvard Business Review*, 2022, 6.

Whittington R, Regner P, Angwin D, Johnson G, and Scholes K (2023). *Exploring Strategy* (13th ed). London, UK: Pearson Education.

Chapter 2

Strategic Decision-Making

Becoming More Strategic

Effective business leaders not only stay around, but they get promoted, lead new ventures, and continue to grow and succeed, but only if their organization succeeds. In healthcare, it's not only about you as an individual leader. It's about the combined vision, direction, and outcomes of the organization overall. On the other hand, you could work for a Fortune 100 company that is consistently top ranked on return on capital or profitability and still fail because of your inability to collaborate or to find common ground with your peers. What separates those that truly lead from those that just manage? The answer: developing a more strategic perspective on decisions they make daily.

To get there, leaders must move beyond the core expertise they came from, whether it's marketing or finance and medical relations or operations. Strategic decisions take a comprehensive look at how choices move the direction of the organization, and the perspective needs to be broad and comprehensive with a focus on the internal values and culture of the team. Leaders consider all broad performance dimensions and not just the financial ones.

Defining Success

Success for each type of healthcare organization might look different based on its profit (or non-profit) status, it's stage of development, it's position

DOI: 10.4324/9781032623726-3

in the community, and the perspectives of the board and executives. Regardless, financial success is typically defined as at least breaking even, but in most cases, growing profitability and revenues year over year. That's hard to do as more companies declare **insolvency** or unable to pay its debt and obligations.

Healthcare bankruptcies increased nearly 84% in 2022 from the prior year, with around 50 healthcare bankruptcies, most of which were pharmaceutical firms and nursing care centers (Bailey, 2023). In addition, new entrants into the market fail nearly 50% of the time within the first 5 years according to the U.S. Bureau of Labor Statistics (BLS, 2023). Most hospitals have negative operating margins. Many retail stores remain highly competitive and are flat in their performance. As part of strategic thinking, we need to consider how to separate the best performers from the rest of the pack. After studying the economics of decision-making for decades, one thing we've learned is that strategy and the results of big decisions we make lead to better outcomes. In essence, it's about leadership and solid decision-making.

Looking at the major health insurance companies (i.e., payers), the average profit margin in 2022 is somewhere between 6% and 10% for most large companies. The largest retail pharmacies, like Walgreens and CVS, hover between 5% and 8% annually. And providers? Well, even the most successful hospitals have close to 0% operating margins, and nearly half have negative operating margins. From a positioning perspective, market segments matter.

Financial performance is just one indicator of a company's value, in addition to quality of care, service, and other indicators of organizational health shown in Chapter 1. But financials are important, and without a margin, mission doesn't matter. Or "no margin, no mission" as it has been colloquialized. And while financials are partially dictated by where an organization is based and who their customers are, a significant portion of performance is based on the management decisions which are made daily. That's why managerial decision-making is so important.

Strategy and Leadership

Let's start with a fundamental premise of business strategy: your decisions—past, present, and future—determine your strategy. In other words, it's not what you say that matters but what you do. Those choices of who to hire, where to open a new location, and what products and areas to invest your limited resources will ultimately become your strategy.

The *Harvard Business Review* examined over 20,000 leaders to identify the six key skills needed for strategic decisions, which they identified as: anticipate, challenge, interpret, decide, align, and learn (Schoemaker et al., 2013). All of these are important, and we'll explore a little more about some of these ideas.

Predict and Anticipate

One of the most complicated aspects of making big decisions is to try to forecast what is coming next, both for your organization and the industry overall. We have excellent hindsight skills, but honing the resources and talent necessary to look forward is complex. Beyond just forecasting, anticipating involves the use of scenarios and reading market signals for clues of what could change—whether that's from a regulatory standpoint, revenue reimbursement, technology, or any other dimension. Strategic-minded executives need to anticipate where the industry is headed and adapt the organization to these changes.

Challenge Existing Mindsets

A difficult task for any senior leader is to change the organization's culture, which is comprised of the collective stories, beliefs, and values that the firm has created. But strategic leaders challenge the status quo and move to change mindsets and beliefs, so that the organization can head in new or different directions. How do you do that if you're the brand-new CEO (chief executive officer) of a retail pharmacy chain or a hospital, with thousands of employees that are engrained in the existing culture and climate? Start by examining your own perspective. Do you bring in new information to a decision or rely on your gut instinct? When teams make decisions do you just agree, or do you challenge their assumptions and ask questions? Do you create dialogue and debate so that team members can openly discuss decisions and topics? If you don't, get on board!

Synthesize and Interpret Confounding Information

Sometimes, in decision-making, we have too little information, but at other times, we might have too much. Both are problematic unless you have the ability to synthesize and interpret confounding information. Let's say your Chief Information Officer recommends implementing a new system, while your Chief Customer Officer recommends no major changes at the present time to improve customer retention. You hear from multiple staff and committees on this subject. All of them are giving you new pieces of data that you should consider. What do you do?

Making decisions typically involves receiving conflicting information from multiple sources, and the better you are at synthesizing it, or condensing it into usable data, the better. Then, interpret the intentions and anticipated outcomes before making a decision.

Seek Alignment within the Organization

Maintaining internal alignment with other members of the leadership team, providers, and staff helps to keep decisions on track. Building alignment is about improving your communication skills, working to become trustworthy and able to extend trust to others, and to honor your commitments. Alignment with the organization's values and direction is equally as important. All choices should be considered with respect to how they move the organization in the intended direction. Keeping internal alignment with the organization is essential to strategic decision-making.

Strategic alignment refers to balancing and maintaining concordance between the mission, vision, strategic objectives, and daily decisions made throughout the organization. Such alignment needs to be within the firm but also with all players and partners in your market segment. If your organization does one thing, and your vendor or regulators do something entirely different, there will be a mismatch and problems will ensue. To create alignment, start with a solid strategic decision-making process.

The Limits of Rationality

When management decision-making theorists began exploring the concept of how professional managers make choices in their companies, they largely pointed to what was called rational methods. Rational implies that a manager has a goal and seeks the one best solution that maximizes their goal. Rational decision-making relies on the use of a structured process that is

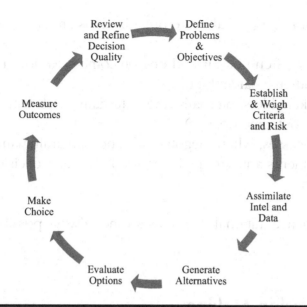

Figure 2.1   Traditional decision-making process.

logically organized and focused, based on reasoning, and intended to help the organization achieve pre-determined expected results. That makes sense in theory. Let's say we want to maximize profits, we would expect a manager to make choices that are aligned with making more money, not less profit. This theory was first described by Herbert Simon (1960), who viewed it as a three-step process:

1. Finding occasions to make a **decision** (or the output of a process, and selection among multiple alternatives)
2. Finding possible courses of action, and
3. Choosing among multiple options.

This traditional decision-making process is shown in Figure 2.1.

Yet, there is one large assumption behind the concept of "rationality", and that is the condition that managers know what their goal is and what solution might get them there the most efficiently. As organizations become large and less coordinated, it is difficult to know what is the "right solution" or even which of the various performance outcomes takes precedent over the others.

In addition, most large healthcare organizations are characterized by:

- goals that are often unclear and one outcome area does not take priority over another (goal ambiguity)
- multiple stakeholders internally and externally, each with a different perspective (outcome opacity)
- political processes, where negotiations and bargaining among multiple departments and groups is required for major decisions (complex organizations)

Therefore, in practice, rational decisions are not always possible or put in practice.

Strategic Decision-Making

Building off the concept of rationality, theories involving strategic management decision-making (SDM) have tried to define what else embodies a strategic choice. **Strategic decision-making** occurs at the highest levels of an organization and typically involves major commitments of resources or changes in strategic direction. Understanding the unique aspects of this industry are important because they have been described as both *service-intensive* (i.e., large labor costs) and *goal-ambiguous* (i.e., helping to improve broad measures of "health"). Management theorists from over 35 years ago, such as Harrison (1987), have suggested that as the organization's environment becomes more complex, there is a higher use of "judgment" in decision-making and less procedural computation as in a rational model of decision-making. This is interesting to note for people trained with quantitative or even clinical backgrounds, who use data and algorithms often to help guide their choices. At the highest levels of an organization, decisions are largely made by instinct and judgment than by analytical process. Bargaining, or strategic negotiations between various actors in the organization, is also commonly found in healthcare.

Strategic decision-making typically involves decision processes that have broad organizational outcomes and are taken by senior management, with implications including major financial commitment of resources. SDM address major organizational issues such as restructuring, new product or service introductions, new facilities, quality, geographic locations, acquisitions, and other organizational changes.

While early theories tell us that rational, analytical, and well-reasoned decisions *should* be made, in practice, the higher the level in an organization that a decision is made, the more subjective and judgmental it becomes. More recently, there has been a strong emphasis on decision-making as a behavioral process, since decisions are made by individuals, where personality and judgment represent both a source of bias and influence on decision processes.

Behavioral theories on decision-making take into account the emotions, feelings, and thoughts of the decider, as well as those that the decision impacts. Decisions generally become more unique and complex as they grow in regard to their importance. A computer or artificial intelligence can solve any problem that has been solved hundreds of times, but the first time a novel problem arises, computers are of little value. You have to learn to rely more on unstructured processes involving judgment and general problem solving, as well as obtaining collaboration and input from multiple sources. This emphasizes behavioral processes since they involve ambiguity, conflict, negotiations, and even bias created by the interaction of individuals and personalities.

Decision-making in healthcare can also be seen as political, where bargaining between individuals in an organization occurs until a satisfactory (not necessarily optimal) decision can be agreed upon. Especially in healthcare, where various medical, legal, business, regulatory, and community input is necessary to make big decisions, bargaining, and collective strategies. **Trade-offs**, or compromises between two or more choices, are very common as well as satisficing (not necessarily achieving the optimal result).

From both the organizational and political perspectives, the concept of "bounded rationality" has emerged. **Bounded rationality** suggests that humans or individuals have only a limited, finite capacity to understand all options available to them and process them in an evaluation mode (Simon, 1979). Bounded rationality can also be described as limits on the human's ability to process and interpret large volumes of data (Bazerman, 2005). Theory suggests that while rational models think all alternatives are known, they usually are not and there is no known probability or consequences of the actions. Also, goals are changing, and the process is not always as sequential as it would appear. Complexity of decision processes is also often used to describe why rational models are not appropriate.

Due to all of these characteristics described, organizational decision-making processes are quite complex and involve multiple frameworks and concepts that leaders should master. Central to all of these is the desire to be more cognitively rational, while using behavioral techniques that involve collaboration, judgment, and bargaining.

Toward a More Behavioral Strategy for Decision-Making

Even with the concept of Lean, flat, or horizontal team-based structures, in most organizations, decisions made at the top of the hierarchy are implemented by those lower in the organization. By that I mean, if the CEO decides on a path or vision, that vision should be supported and enacted by decisions made by her leadership team and subordinates. This isn't always the case, but there must be **structural alignment**, or coordination and collaboration, between the vision with operational decisions.

Strategy should lead decision-making. Decisions nearly always involve some degree of change, and a commitment to allocating resources to those choices usually follow. That's what makes decisions effective. Yet, behavior often gets in our way.

No matter how much we want to take attitudes, emotions, feelings, and thoughts out of organizational decision-making, it is nearly impossible to extract or sever ourselves from certain situations. We all have complex emotions and behaviors, so no matter how rational or analytical we try to be, we might have a bias one way or another, or strong negative or positive feelings for one alternative over another. Emotions and behaviors also impact our relationships with our management team, staff, medical providers, and customers. This is normal, and why we don't always act rational even as organizations.

Organizations have to shift focus to the design of behaviorally informed decision processes and create strategy that is based on firm and individual behaviors (Sibony et al., 2017). Consider the case of how your own personality and moods impact your perspective and worldview. Your mood on any given day might affect how you review a restaurant you visit, or the traffic you face on your commute. A bad mood might damper your perspective, and therefore any choices that follow could also be impacted accordingly. This happens both individually and collectively in organizations.

Collectively, in organizations, the emotions and moods of the team impact culture and climate. This in turn impacts how we lead and how we choose. The best way to deal with this is for each leader to recognize the mood and emotions you face when deciding or choosing a path in your organization and remind yourself of the goals and objectives you are trying to pursue. Do a check to make sure these behaviors aren't swaying your decisions in that moment. We will discuss much more about behaviors in the chapter on leadership.

Re-Framing Decision-Making

When making decisions, consider your decision **inputs** to the process. Inputs are information that are used in processing to assess how one should make a decision. Inputs are both controllable (they are within your control) and uncontrollable (you can't change these). Inputs involve data received from your team or customers for example but also requirements placed on you by procurement or legal for example.

An input includes both long- and short-term objectives for the company, such as where you are headed, and when and how you want to get there. These need to serve as drivers of the choices if possible. Focus on these when processing decision, as well as intelligence about market trends, competitors, and any other inputs you have.

Decisions involve organizational change. No matter how you look at it, any big decision will require resources to be spent in that direction over another. It requires mobilization of staff to focus on that initiative. Because of this, all decisions involve altering direction, culture, and might also create tension within the organization. It's important to manage that change appropriately so that there is internal alignment, less friction, and more support for the decisions.

Strategic decisions also involve high levels of uncertainty. Regardless of how "certain" you feel that if you do one thing, it will result in a specific outcome, there are probabilities involved that can change the calculus. There are no certainties in big decisions. They all involve risk. Estimate probabilities of success, prepare scenarios of what other outcomes might evolve, weigh these alternatives, and then execute accordingly. Take into account that all decisions are **stochastic** (based on chance and probabilities) and not guaranteed or deterministic. With strategic decisions, you can't control everything, and random chances will likely lead to different outcomes.

In thinking about the decision, it is usually best to evaluate what the best outcome (or utility or value) that the decision will bring. Consider that best option as well as a most likely and an unfavorable outcome so that you can understand all possibilities. Consider that outcomes are gauged by multiple perspectives. Are outcomes measured by what it looks like on surface, or at face value? Do you just compare potential solutions to one another and choose the best? Or do you just analyze the outcome based on how it was obtained? How comprehensively you researched it, collaborated, and sought involvement from others? We won't know the outcome of a choice for some time. Especially strategic choices. So, focus more on the latter and not the former. That would entail what we call **decision quality**. Decision quality refers to how good the process was when making a decision, irrespective of the actual outcome. So, you can have a really bad outcome, but if you made the choice with all the right inputs, had good research and intelligence, and took your time analyzing the options, then the decision quality would still be high.

But keep in mind also, who is evaluating the outcome? Is the outcome being viewed only from your perspective? If so, we as humans are very likely to over-estimate the effectiveness of our choice. We usually are biased positively in favor of our own choices. Or are the patient or customers evaluating the decisions? Or, your Board of Directors, or your leadership team? Depending on who is evaluating the decision outcome, will determine how "successful" the choice really was in their unique perspective, regardless of the quality.

There are many trade-offs with decision-making. This means, at times, you might have to choose one attribute over another (e.g., better features over the lowest price). We typically make trade-offs between efficiency and service levels. Higher levels of service typically imply a little lower efficiency. Consider the example of an over-the-counter (OTC) medication on a retail pharmacy shelf. Having too much of it (higher level of service for potential customers) might mean lower efficiency (higher carrying cost, more shelf space occupied). Consider all trade-offs when making strategic decisions.

Finally, once a big decision is made, remember that the work doesn't stop there. You need to cultivate a climate within your organization where that decision can be welcomed warmly, accepted, and made successful. The use of change management techniques, education, and collaboration with your leadership team and the staff is equally as important to SDM effectiveness.

Case 2.1: Dogma Medical Group

Dogma Medical Group is a physician-owned group practice employing nearly 1,000 staff across the Midwest U.S. The firm was started with one goal—to allow physicians freedom to make medical decisions and care in line with best clinical practices, regardless of financial implications. At times, this has resulted in significant expenses that are greater than revenues earned for each case, but the quality of care has remained exceptional. Customers (i.e., patients) have expressed their gratitude for the highest level of care imaginable. Yet, the current managing director (Tom Reyonds, CEO) comes from a for-profit hospital system and would like to make the practice more profitable. Tom instituted a process of using Lean and Six Sigma techniques to improve process efficiency and is now requiring the Purchasing department's approval for all expenses greater than $500. Physicians, the collective ownership group, are furious and are considering leaving. There is significant lack of alignment, and decision processes have become bureaucratic. How should the CEO try to resolve the situation he has created?

Steps toward Strategic Decisions

To unravel decision-making, think about these simple steps.

1. Create a long-term direction and strategic plan. Create a plan that established your direction and objectives. Make decisions that are in line with this plan daily.
2. Systematize your decision-making. This involves ensuring key performance outcomes and objectives are being considered at the onset of a choice. Then, establish decision rules and parameters around who can make what type of decision and the dollar amount. Be consistent in use of teams, communication, and alignment when making decisions.
3. Understand your competitors and market intelligence when making a strategic decision. Know that any real big decision will either be emulated or matched by competitors and stay aligned with a strategy based on uniqueness and differentiation. Invest in resources that can help get you market-based information.
4. Strengthen your leadership and your team. It's important to continue to develop your team, identify gaps in skills, and use strategic recruitment to fill voids in the leadership team.
5. Build a better relationship with your board of advisers or directors. Work on improving communications with the board and allowing boards to become more active in certain areas. Even if you are not a C-suite executive, you can still learn what board members are interested

in, where they would like the organization to head, and how you can play a role in that.

6. Make your operations more resilient and implement plans flawlessly. Besides labor, your supply chain is likely your second biggest expense. It needs to be carefully fortified and built to be resilient. Most importantly, a decision doesn't stop at the choice—it must be executed, or operationalized, and that involves follow-through, commitment, and internal alignment on smaller decisions and timelines.

7. Monitor and manage your key strategic performance indicators. Using analytics and scorecard metrics for strategic management is essential to staying in alignment and improving all measures of organizational health.

We will focus much more on all of these concepts throughout subsequent chapters.

Chapter Summary

- Rational decision-making theories have evolved into more behaviorally informed strategic approach.
- Outlining your organization's key goals is essential to making more rational decisions that are in line with the purpose and the positioning for the firm.
- Alignment is important in so many areas when making strategic decisions. Be sure to include your organizational partners (e.g., vendors, distributors, customers) and key players (e.g., regulators, stakeholders) when making decisions to maintain alignment.
- Successful leaders should master skills related to better anticipating the future, challenging current mindsets, interpreting complex and comprehensive information, aligning their staff and organization, and learning from what is working and what is not.

Discussion Questions

1. If you were to make a big decision to acquire a new facility (a new store, clinic, or company for example), what would be the best ways to consider potential options?

2. What internal sources of intelligence might you call on to gain insights into that organization?
3. Consider a recent big decision you have made for your organization. Evaluate the decision quality from multiple perspectives, as well as its outcomes.

Key Terms

Bounded Rationality; Decision; Decision Quality; Inputs; Stochastic; Strategic Decision-Making; Trade-Offs

References

Bailey V (2023). Healthcare Bankruptcies Grew by 84% in 2022, Returning to 2020 Levels. *Revenue Cycle Intelligence*. Jan 19, 2023. Available at https://revcycleintelligence.com/news/healthcare-bankruptcies-grew-by-84-in-2022-returning-to-2020-levels

BLS (2023). U.S. Bureau of Labor Statistics. Entrepreneurship and the U.S. Economy. Accessed November 10, 2023. Available at https://www.bls.gov/bdm/entrepreneurship/entrepreneurship.htm

Schoemaker PJ, Krupp S, and Howland S (2013). Strategic leadership: the essential skills. *Harvard Business Review*, 91, 131–134.

Sibony O, Lovallo D, and Powell TC (2017). Behavioral strategy and the strategic decision architecture of the firm. *California Management Review*, 59(3), 5–21.

Chapter 3

Strategic Intelligence

The real value of an effective strategy process is based on the quality of the inputs. If the information in the internal and external analyses is not sufficiently relevant, timely, comprehensive, or futuristic, the strategies designed will be ineffective. You've probably heard of the terminology "garbage in, garbage out".

Effective strategic analysis requires in-depth research that goes beyond superficial levels. For example, traditional planning data for hospitals includes such measures as average age of the population in the markets served, which drives the types of services that hospitals should perform and what level of resources are required to support these efforts. Drilling into this further, an organization might use statistical modeling to discover that average age of patients has had little impact on services performed in their marketplace.

Although there are dozens of tools and techniques discussed in strategic analysis, they are all considered part of the larger subject of strategic intelligence. Use this chapter as a guide for jump-starting an intelligence program and system at your organization.

What is Strategic Intelligence?

Strategy and decision-making is best if used with information that can help the decision-maker be fully informed (Langabeer, 1998). This is easier for personal decisions than complex organizational ones, but it can be accomplished. **Strategic intelligence** is much more than having reams of paper

 DOI: 10.4324/9781032623726-4

or complex data reports, it involves systematizing your decisions to enable long-term organizational success. A strong system for gathering intelligence can provide a wealth of insights into your competitors' strategies, products, and messaging, as well as your own business insights. It helps give you the knowledge you need to stay one step ahead in the market. In this chapter, we will discuss how to create a system for strategic intelligence.

Strategic intelligence are data points used in making better decisions and formulating more effective strategy. This process involves collecting, processing, analyzing, and disseminating essential bits of information needed to establish organizational policies and strategies. The types of information typically centers around:

■ Competitors and markets (**competitive intelligence**)
■ Internal financials and performance (business intelligence)
■ Industry analyses and rankings (industry intelligence)
■ Risks, threats, and mitigation plans (security intelligence)

What sets successful companies apart is their ability to leverage intelligence as a continual process and not a one-time task. Staying ahead of the game requires constant monitoring, analysis, and adaptation and is key to unlocking new opportunities and ensuring your company's long-term success in a highly competitive market.

To formulate really effective strategy, decisions have to be based on sound underlying data about the industry, your competitors, future plans, and your own internal capabilities (Kolbe and Morrow, 2022). This is called intelligence. We use intelligence and research to form data-driven decisions. What do we mean specifically by intelligence? Intelligence is all about acquiring, managing, and analyzing *knowledge*. Acquiring, or gathering, this intelligence is usually the most challenging.

Knowledge about your industry and market (market research), competitors (competitive analysis), and even supplier intelligence can help you to figure out what you're missing. Regardless of the nature of the intelligence, the process is quite similar.

Strategic Intelligence Framework

There are five activities within the intelligence framework, as seen in Figure 3.1. We will review each of these in the sections that follow.

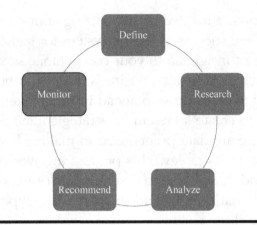

Figure 3.1   Intelligence framework.

Intelligence Parameters: Defining Intentions and Framing the Objectives

Intelligence is like a puzzle, with each piece of data representing a part of your competitor's strategy. It's about gathering and analyzing information on everything from their social media presence to their pricing and service line or product strategy and using it to create a complete picture of their potential next moves. With strong competitive intelligence analysis, you can supercharge your strategy and make informed decisions that drive success. So, if you want to stay ahead of the game, competitive intelligence is the key to unlocking a winning strategy.

Healthcare executives have a variety of decisions they must make. These decisions range from the strategic to the operational. Each decision poses a problem that needs to be resolved. Competitive intelligence should be used to address these problems. Here is a sample of problems, issues, or business decisions that might need competitive intelligence:

- What hospitals or other clinical facilities would make good acquisition candidates?
- What is the underlying need and economics for a proposed new clinical service line?
- How does our hospital compare in terms of costs, quality, and performance to others?
- Are our faculty practitioners as "productive" or "efficient" as Hospital X's practitioners?
- What degree of integration exists in our competing networks?
- What new programs or facilities are our competitors considering?

These are just a sample of problems which competitive intelligence will be able to help resolve. In the course of daily decision-making or periodic strategic planning, issues such as these arise. The standard response is to use "gut feel" or intuition to make decisions. The competitive intelligence process attempts to make more scientific or informed decisions through more comprehensive information.

Once the problems have been identified, the problem needs to be "framed". Specifically, framing the problem requires the CI (competitive intelligence) analyst to decipher the components of the problem in order to understand how to go about solving it. Let's look at the following scenario.

Assume that a large urban teaching hospital is considering adding a new clinical service line in the internal medicine service line. The hospital administrator evaluates the department's business plan and finds that there is plenty of data about the medical conditions and potential for research funding, but little information about competing services from neighboring hospitals and financial viability. Since the presence of competition will impact the intensity of third-party payer bargaining power, the administrator determines she needs more intelligence. Recognizing the need for more comprehensive information is the first step in the intelligence process. With this new assignment, an analyst further defines and frames the problems more extensively, such as: Are there any other local competitor's providing this service line? Where is the nearest facility which provides this service? How many cases have they performed in the last year? Are health plans interested in adding another provider for this service? What types of discounts might we expect? Each of these questions, and probably many more, will have to be fully explored.

Defining and framing the problem requires an analytical mind that can understand the problem, help to determine exactly what the decision-maker is looking for, determine the number of answers desired, and then identify potential sources of the information. All of this is required before going on to the second step in the process: collecting data.

This first step involves defining the goals and objectives for the intelligence you are looking for. Are you trying to find optimal prices, or data on your market? Are you looking to explore competitors latest releases of a product, or facilities and launches in new markets? Or are you trying to be broad across all areas of competition, markets, industry, and risks? Clearly define these broad goals, and if possible, narrow down to specifically stated objectives to help you gather the right data. For example, "…to learn more about competitor X plans to start a new service line in a specific region".

Conducting Intelligence Research

The second activity in the framework involves performing the research and investigation. Start by solidifying which sources to pull from and then start collecting. In healthcare, there are an endless variety of data sources which can be of use to strategy analysts, ranging from print to electronic formats and from basic to creative sources. Often, specialized tools and databases can be helpful as well. When it comes to CI tools and resources, businesses must consider their specific needs and budget. By far, the most widely available and fastest growing source of data is the internet. The internet has seen an explosion of excellent healthcare news and data sources over the last couple of years. Social media monitoring software can also provide valuable insights, and larger companies may require more advanced software with sophisticated features.

For certain projects, data will not be published and available through secondary sources such as periodicals and the internet. For these types of situations, analysts must use creative data sources. Primary data can be collected through observations of competitor processes, interviews with external parties and competitor's customers, market research, or the use of focus groups. For example, if you needed to know what types of new programs are being considered at a competing hospital, consider scouring the job postings for physicians in medical journals. Creative data sources are often more time-consuming and resource-intensive, but the use of such primary research tools are often required to address certain strategic issues.

There are multiple specialized and proprietary data sources in existence which can be useful in intelligence-building. These include, but are not limited to, the following:

- Published analyst reports (e.g., Hoovers, D&B, Gartner) or any industry-specific research from trade publications such as Becker's Healthcare, Modern Healthcare, and many others.
- If you are examining public companies, look for published 10K or 10Q financial statements and reports which often give forecasts and background on potential strategies.
- If you are examining non-profits, look at prior year tax returns on GuideStar (guidestar.org) or the American Hospital Directory (AHD.com).

■ Conduct an internet search to see what forward-looking quotes and statements have been offered to the media by the CEO or other executives.

■ Consider conducting intelligence gathering from customers or clients, as well as your current employees. Your employees are aware of much more than just your products and services, and likely, they use others as well.

■ Try targeting sales and business development staff of other firms for brief interviews or focus groups.

■ Examine competitor's websites and the social media of leaders from those organizations.

■ Investigate proprietary databases owned by the organization or put together by others.

■ Search all prior news articles, white papers, and reports from secondary sources.

Analyzing the Data: Making Sense of the Information

Analyzing your competitors' data is where the magic happens—turning raw numbers into valuable insights that can inform your business strategy. But it's not as simple as just looking at a spreadsheet of numbers and making decisions based on that. Analyzing the data requires a deep understanding of your industry, your competitors, and the market as a whole.

One of the first steps in analyzing the data is to look for patterns and trends. What do the numbers tell you about your competitors' performance over time? Are there any fluctuations that can be attributed to specific events or changes in the market? This information can help you anticipate future trends and make informed decisions about your own business strategy.

Another important aspect of analyzing the data is to look for areas where your competitors are underperforming. Are there gaps in their offerings that you could fill? Are there areas where their messaging is weak, or their branding is ineffective? Look at revenue-based market share and customer overlap. From there, narrow down your list to the top competitors—those that are most like your business in terms of value proposition, market share, and offerings. By doing so, you can gain a deep understanding of your competitors' strategies, strengths, and weaknesses, allowing you to stay one step ahead in the marketplace. By identifying these weaknesses, you can capitalize on them and gain a competitive advantage.

Once the data is collected relevant to address the objective, the raw data will need to be analyzed or modeled. Sometimes, there will be a need for quantitative methods, such as econometrics or statistical regression, and other times, the analysis phase will only involve filtering the data for inconsistencies and significance. In almost all cases however, this analytical stage is the linchpin that helps convert data into intelligence.

Here are some specific types of analyses that are conducted.

- *Financial Analysis*: Financial analyses are used when an executive wants to know how a specific unit or the entire organization performs relative to other "best in class" facilities. Detailed financial models about competitor's working capital, liquidity, efficiency, and profitability are all standard metrics. Common ratios that are used for these purposes include return on assets (operating margin divided by total assets) and debt to equity ratio (total debt to total equity or fund balance). Additionally, financial analyses are used by CI analysts to estimate projected cash inflows for specific service lines that are being considered for strategic investment within the hospital.
- *Forecasting*: Speed and time offer distinct competitive advantages. In order to improve timing, by knowing when and how to execute plans, forecasting is often used to enhance strategy execution. Forecasting can be used to predict future performance, to project healthcare demand or needs for certain services in the future, or to estimate the amount of resources to invest in specific programs. Enhanced use of integrated business forecasting can be used to improve a number of strategic decisions, including marketing promotion, capital budgeting, and even cash management applications. Various forecasting techniques include the neural networks, Bayesian methods, Delphi technique, linear trends, exponential smoothing, and the Box-Jenkins technique.
- *Process Mapping*: Many projects require an understanding of how a competitor's networks operate or perform in the context of your own organization or facility. Process mapping requires an analyst to flow-chart the details of the series of step-by-step activities, from start to finish, within a process. Process mapping can be used to compare the referral process within a competing network, the process for patient scheduling, or simply mapping the relationship within the network. Process mapping is extremely useful for understanding how your competitors execute their plans relative to your organization.

■ *Benchmarking*: Benchmarking is the process of seeking and learning from the best practices of other organizations, with the intention of applying those to your own organization. Benchmarking involves three primary steps: (1) Find the appropriate hospitals to benchmark against. Typically, the hospital with best practices can be discovered through write-ups in hospital news journals, or by analyzing the competition's financial or quality performance; (2) Determine what makes their performance differential, through interviews and research. Although it may be difficult to get competing hospitals in different networks to discuss their processes, interviews with their patients, payers, and direct observations can all be used to evaluate what is making them differential; and (3) Apply those learnings to your own hospital to improve performance. After discovering what is making another company successful, the organization should look to adapt these findings to their own unique environment and try to make them a source of differential performance. As health continues to work in strategic alliances, benchmarking within these networks should be high on your priority. Often there are best practices right there in your own backyard.

■ *Statistical Models*: Statistical models are often helpful to determine which factors are contributing to achieving a certain outcome. The most common statistical technique used is multiple linear regression, which identifies variables that in combination have the most influence on a specific outcome (i.e., the dependent variable) across a broad number of observations. Regressions are used in many academic studies, and in large industry models, and are used widely to determine what organizational strategies or practices help to improve financial performance. The statistical analyses supporting the strategies for organizations suggested in Chapter 3 used regression for its robustness and accuracy. With modern technology, even the most sophisticated regressions can be run on a personal computer using any number of software programs, including SPSS, SAS, Stata, and StatGraphics.

■ *Scenario Models*: For strategic planning purposes, strategists are often asked to help estimate a vision of what the future will hold. Scenario models represent collective insight into likely or probable scenarios that might play out relative to the issues being researched. Scenarios represent one method of managing the uncertainty of the future.

■ *Game Theory*: Game theory requires strategists to evaluate how competition will respond to specific strategies or moves made by the hospital. The term "game" implies that this type of analytical tool can be used in planning "war rooms" or laboratories and do not actually require hospitals to implement them in practice. Strategies applied in the wrong environment or against motivated competitors can be costly mistakes. Game theory helps to take the guess work out of strategies by systematically playing out each strategy, estimating how the competitor will respond, and then evaluating the payoff. The strategy with the best outcome is the one that should be used. CI analysts are often used to build the framework for the game, secure the data, and facilitate the process. Here is how it would work. Assume that an organization wants to understand the impact of a certain complex decision, such as the elimination of a particular service line or a specific advertising campaign. A hospital would assemble the planning team or other working group. The team would then divide up into a couple of sub-teams to simulate the hospital, its competitors, and external participants such as the local media or payers. The hospital sub-team would roll out the strategy, and each sub-team would discuss their perspectives, issues, and potential defensive strategies to employ. Many iterations and sequences take place, as the teams continue to create new strategies in response to competitive maneuvers. The interactions in this game, and the insights learned from the various perspectives can be extremely insightful and can help to ensure that the strategies are well formulated and comprehensive before they are deployed. Although game theory can be highly complex and quantitative, real value can be gained by organizations that employ them in any fashion.

■ *Simulation*: When a game is played dynamically with a computer program that can simulate the real world, it becomes a simulation. Simulations allow games to be played out fast, with excellent what-if capabilities. Many consulting firms have developed computer simulations that can help organizations test their competitive strategies before they are actually rolled out. Simulation is excellent for examining the quantitative impact of strategic decisions when there are high costs involved with errors, unfamiliar problems, and complex situations.

All of these analytical tools can be used in this third step of the intelligence process.

Recommend and Monitor

The last two steps involve recommending a path forward based on your assessments and then continuing to follow-up and monitor changes in any of the intelligence sources. Monitoring and continuous feedback loops to update intelligence as it changes is necessary at all times, to avoid making decisions that are no longer based on facts. Strategic planning analyst, market analyst, or CI analysts are great staff roles that can help support better strategic leadership.

In order to comprehensively understand the interactions with each of these competitors, an intelligence system needs to be created and updated continuously. This system should be some form of database that can capture the most current transactions, details, and events with regard to the competition. Each project that a CI analyst performs on a competitor needs to be maintained in this extensive intelligence system in order to continuously track the strategic maneuvers of all competitors.

An intelligence system should possess at least five key components. It should have: (1) Current factual details on key competitors, such as size, revenues, market share, number of service lines, and names of key personnel; (2) Summary of competitor's strategies, key strengths and weaknesses, and other relevant strategic data; (3) Market data, such as number of locations and facilities, customer or payer mix, specific market segments, and overall supply and demand by market; (4) Transactional events and data on both the market and competition obtained through intelligence efforts and projects conducted by analysts; and (5) Risks and threats that are discovered during the process of collecting intelligence. An intelligence system helps to ensure that the latest and most comprehensive information is at the decision-maker's disposal when they need it.

Recommendations are easier to provide if you are the CEO who did the intelligence yourself. But if you are a staff member or manager preparing a report for senior leaders or the board, you will need to package a report to deliver with your recommendations. As you package the report, consider these tips:

■ Follow a simple outline: Objective, Background, Facts, and Recommendations.
■ Summarize the objective of your intelligence gathering with clear statements of the goals and objectives you used in this process. Similar to

the concept of decision quality, the intel you gather will be evaluated based on how you achieved or didn't the goals of the process.

■ Use concise, short message statements of fact, without interpretation in a background section to describe what you found with good statistics if possible.

■ Recommendations are what follows, which are the intelligence analyst can make suggestions as to the right path forward based on all that you have analyzed.

■ Keep the entire package short but have available to any decision-maker all of the specific detailed data if they need it, as well as sources and references. Most "chief" or C-level employees do not have time or capacity to read extensive reports, so keep it short and simple with the right amount of detail to convey all knowledge garnered from the process.

Case 3.1: Aurora Health CMO

Fran Anavole is the Chief Marketing Officer of an urban health system called Aurora Health, who is tasked with assessing which location in a nearby suburb would be best for a new hospital facility. The board of directors and the CEO is trying to grow health system revenues by 25% over the next 5 years and have decided a regional expansion would be the best strategy to achieve that. She sets her objective as identifying target locations based on population growth and presence of competitors.

She realizes that something is missing. Does she want to replicate existing patient demographics in the new location, or try to make changes to target customers? She also doesn't fully understand what payer mix is best for this expansion. Does Aurora Health want more cash pay, commercial insurance, or some other segment? There is much more than understanding demographics and competitor presence required to gather this intelligence.

She decides to assemble a small team to define what the variables are for making an optimal choice. The team quickly comes back with a need to focus on obstetrics, to make strategic use of their world-class physicians in OB/GYN, and close proximity to the clinics managed by their partner at the local medical school. With this new set of information, Fran has a much better idea of how to proceed with her intelligence assessment.

Chapter Summary

■ Intelligence involves knowledge necessary to allow healthcare executives to address specific issues or problems at hand. Understanding and categorizing competitor's actions are a necessary component of this.

■ A focus on strategic intelligence will help organizations become more market-driven and more rigorous in their analytical process.

■ Leaders must empower their intelligence teams to gather resources comprehensively, and to monitor for changes and threats continuously.

■ The basic intelligence process involves five steps: define the objectives, conduct the research, analyze the data, make recommendations and disseminate to decision makers, and then monitor and follow-up. Capturing these findings in an intelligence system will help organizations remain current on the market and competition.

■ Strategic intelligence about the nature of your competitors, market, industry, and risks are about improving strategic planning and strategic decision-making. Be sure to integrate the knowledge gained from the continuous intelligence framework to help deliver better strategic thinking.

Discussion Questions

1. Competitor intelligence is probably the most common way that strategic knowledge is collected for management. Does your organization have an individual or team in place to help you continuously examine the competition and the markets?
2. Identification of potential risks and threats from new entrants or substitute products and services is a key area of intelligence gathering. What discovery has your intelligence team found that led to changes in strategic plans or process?
3. What area of your organization could benefit most from more in-depth research and knowledge? Identify a couple of areas and consider assigning a workgroup to look at intelligence gathering.

Key Terms

Competitive Intelligence; Strategic Intelligence

References

Kolbe PR and Morrow MR (2022). How corporate intelligence teams help businesses manage risk. *Harvard Business Review*, January 4, 2022. Available at https://hbr.org/2022/01/how-corporate-intelligence-teams-help-businesses-manage-risk

Langabeer JR (1998). Achieving a strategic focus for competitive intelligence. *Competitive Intelligence Review*, 9(1), 55–59.

Chapter 4

Strategic Planning

Strategic planning focuses on possibilities and alternatives involving an uncertain future. For that reason alone, planning is essential to better strategic thinking. In this chapter, we will start with the basics. First, all organizations—both for-profit and non-profit—need a strategic plan. This does *not* mean some extensive bound report that sits on a shelf, but rather a strategic plan is a roadmap that defines your key decisions, including where you are headed and how you will get there. If your company's direction and performance were already determined (or deterministic as we say), there would be no reason to plan. But, given the high state of uncertainty (since ultimately, the future is unknowable), strategic planning provides executives and decision-makers the time and mental flexibility to ponder "what if" on a variety of fronts.

In board rooms across the globe, owners and leaders contemplate their future and determine what products to offer, what locations to serve, and what partners to collaborate with. It helps to set revenue targets, define new geographical priorities, and to re-examine where your priorities lay.

There are five stages of strategic planning that don't need to be over-complicated. There is no need to make it annual only, or too complex. Just focus on what you really need out of the plan: direction, unique value proposition, and performance expectations. Here are the five steps we recommend and will describe.

1. *Goal Setting*: In this phase, you need to assign members of your team and develop strategic goals so that structure is provided to the proc. If you have an advisory board, use them for this process. Develop

DOI: 10.4324/9781032623726-5

timelines (when you need some input) and goals (what are your metrics?). You should be preparing your decision-making needs for the activities you're going to go through.

2. *Incorporate Your Intelligence*: In this phase, think of data and market research collection. You want to focus on analyzing your historical data, especially during the last year. Analyze trends. Are you seeing any changes by customer segment? Any decrease in funding in a specific service line? Analyze the data in several ways, to try to yield intelligence about what is happening. You're looking to examine what is happening with your operations and outcomes. Work with your sales and marketing team to refine a revenue forecast. Your accounting folks can help look at expense forecasts and profitability. The goal in this phase is to come up with some clear sense of how your business is shifting, if any, and in what area.

3. *Assess Your Environment*: Think outside your four walls. Here you want to think through your outside influencers, such as new regulations or laws, changes in economic structure (such as changes in inflation or stock markets), and other areas outside-your-control (e.g., think about the impact COVID-19 had on all industries). Despite your best efforts, you are most likely to not meet your expectations if you have a high level of market concentration (or competition). Focus on all aspects of your external (non-organizational) components, such as customer, competitors, industry, and environment. Address questions such as:

   – What motivates customers to buy products or to seek service within the specific industry?
   – How might changing demographics impact future demand?
   – What attributes of the product and service are important?
   – What valued-added services, product options, extras, and components are desirable?
   – What objectives do customers seek?
   – What changes in motivation are occurring or could occur?
   – Are customers dissatisfied with any specific areas?
   – Are there any unmet needs or things your competitors can't provide?

4. *Develop Strategic Alternatives*: You should be starting to see some general patterns. At this stage, brainstorm the strategic alternatives or alternative paths forward. What are your primary choices (or decisions), and which ones are most important to your future? Weigh everything in terms of their anticipated performance effect, such as sales growth,

Figure 4.1 Planning process.

profitability, or other metrics you might have. Think less about the consequences and more about the impact.

5. *Flawlessly Execute*: The first four steps focus on strategy formulation, and this final step is all about delivery. Flawless execution we call it, where strategies get put into practice. You should think through potential changes to the management team, to pricing, to locations, to internal shifting of the budget, to use of consultants, and to strategic hires for key positions. Consider developing a short list of strategies, after addressing these kinds of questions. Executing the strategic plan is often the most difficult part of strategic planning because there are so many things beyond our control.

Figure 4.1 presents a summary diagram of the planning process. Next, we'll dive into each of these topics.

Strategic Planning

Strategic planning is the process by which strategies are developed or formulated and alternative directions are conceived. Strategic planning as a concept has ebbed and flowed in popularity (Mintzberg, 1994). In strategy, the focus is on alignment between the changing needs of the external environment and the capabilities of the internal organization. A leader may want to quadruple their size, but if they don't have the financial or human resources to carry that out, there is a lack of alignment. The outcome of successful strategic planning is collaboration around direction, differentiation, and decisions on how to adapt to changing healthcare dynamics. This chapter will define steps necessary for a thorough strategic planning process.

Planning is one of the basic management functions required for any organization to survive. Strategic planning involves mapping the external opportunities and threats with the internal strengths and weaknesses to define strategic alternatives and stake out an appropriate competitive position. The output of strategic planning is typically a plan that defines the specific functional strategies to employ for each dimension of business strategy.

Despite the fact that planning is about defining strategy, the *process* of strategic planning is more important than the *product*—the strategic plan. The process is important in that it provides the organization with shared concepts about the market, competition, changing technologies, and overall direction. The process allows for mutual discovery of information and should bring consensus among a wide variety of stakeholders. One of the more important results of strategic planning should be consensus among executives about where the organization is headed and how it is going to get there, such as which product markets to invest in and focus on. This shared vision of future direction and goals is essential for success in turbulent environments.

Preparation

Prior to beginning any formal planning process, critical issues about how to organize the planning efforts have to be addressed (Langabeer and Napiewocki, 2000). Choices have to be made about planning team composition, facilitation, timing, resources, and use of strategic analysis tools. When choosing the team, keep in mind that leaders should balance the representation from important groups but also that these individuals will be helping to decide the organization's future. Select people that are fair but also forward-thinking, creative, and energetic. Leaders also need to think about who will facilitate the meetings, and how they will be run. Some companies prefer outside management consultants, while others rely on self-directed teams. Team facilitation styles should fit within your culture and intentions. Also consider the resources necessary for this team to accomplish its charge, to help support benchmarking trips, databases, or consulting fees for example. Finally, preparation should outline the use of any strategic tools that might help in the process.

Incorporate Intelligence

The planning team should make use of all available strategic intelligence, as discussed in Chapter 3. We won't repeat that information, but all intelligence needs to flow into the planning process, including data on your competitors, threats of new entrants, and substitutes.

Assess the External Environment

The second overall step in the strategic planning process requires gathering and analyzing external and internal environmental forces. Externally, we care most about (1) competitors, (2) customers and market/industry, and (3) the legal, regulatory, and technology environment. Customer analyses should focus on the needs of patients, clients, or buyers and the changing requirements that might be forthcoming. It's important to look at how new and existing competitors are evolving to meet these needs. In healthcare, you will see direct care being provided by retail pharmacies (called downstream integration) and also expansion of technologies and other modalities by providers. There is a blurring of typical competitor lines, and so, it's important to fully identify all competitors in your industry. It is possible to serve multiple clients across multiple geographic markets and industries.

Also examine specific **market segments**, which is the targeting of specific customers in the market. Focus on product and service needs, and benefits that are being sought after. You can also examine customer needs by geography, lifestyle, sex, age, income, usage levels, size, or application.

When performing customer analyses, focus on the changes in both buyer behavior and motivation. Ask the team to identify answers to the following questions, such as:

■ Are customers satisfied?
■ Are there unmet needs that need to be addressed?
■ What motivates customers to come to your facilities?
■ What attributes of the care are important?
■ What value-added services, in addition to the actual delivery of care, are desirable?
■ What changes in motivation are occurring or could occur?

Examining customer, competitor, and industry forces can help you create better strategy. In Appendix 1, we provide a checklist of questions that can be addressed in the environmental assessment (Figure 4.2).

When performing a competitive assessment, focus on getting answers to these questions, such as:

■ Who are all competitors we face in our markets?
■ How many competitors are there? How concentrated is the market?
■ How strong a foothold do they have on the market?

Figure 4.2   Competitor assessment.

- Why are competitors able to sustain market share?
- Which competitors should we focus our attentions on? What are their strengths?
- What plans do our competitors have for the short and long term?
- How effective are our competitors' systems and networks?

Successful business strategies focus on understanding your competitor's strengths and competitive positioning and find a way to reduce their effectiveness. Find gaps and exploit (or take advantage of) these weaknesses and opportunities.

Assess the Internal Environment

Now, focus efforts on understanding the opportunities and threats facing your own organization. What skills are missing? What resources do you need? What are the organization's primary limitations? What areas have you been avoiding that might be good to consider? All of these are important considerations. Internal assessments need to focus on your current strategies, historical performance, growth, leadership style, and resource availability. Each of these components help to shape the internal competencies of the organization.

Conduct a SWOT Analysis

Once the external and internal environments have been defined, they need to be aligned or matched against each other. **SWOT** (or strengths, weaknesses, opportunities, and threats) is a type of analysis used to understand your organization and the industry overall. Strengths are the capabilities and competencies at which your organization excels at and should be used to exploit the opportunities available in the market environment, and competitor's weaknesses exposed during the external analysis should become key components of the grand strategy. Weaknesses identified internally within your own organization should be fortified or strengthened, either by investing more resources into those areas or eliminating them altogether.

This combination of strengths, weaknesses, opportunities, and threats generates more questions which have to be addressed to match strategy to your situation. Here are a few questions which have to be considered:

Opportunities: Opportunities are untapped areas of the external environment that represent possibilities for strategic growth. What strengths exist internally to capitalize on the opportunities in the market? How much resources will be required to pursue them? Will we have to increase, reduce, or maintain investments into certain service lines or programs? Will, or have, our competitors already moved on these opportunities? What can we do to thwart their efforts?

Threats: Threats refer to external forces that threaten your ability to perform at desired levels. Threats and risks are used interchangeably and describe potential exposures that may cause harm. Make a list of all industry threats. Are these threats real? How can we mitigate or avoid them?

Strengths: Strengths are our internal set of capabilities which exceed those of our competitors. How can we use our strengths to achieve a greater competitive advantage? How can we block our competitor's service line success by building on our strengths? Should we build these competencies further by continuing investments, or should we be investing resources elsewhere? Will these strengths be enough to achieve an advantage?

Weaknesses: Weaknesses are our organization's internal set of challenges that limit our potential. How can we prevent competitors from exploiting our weaknesses? Can we invest resources into these areas to convert them into strengths, or at least make them neutral? Will these weaknesses prevent us from pursuing certain opportunities?

Generate Strategic Alternatives

Step 4 of the planning process should focus on generating strategic options. The data from the intelligence assessments and the environmental analyses should help guide the organization. Many people find that the use of Delphi techniques, brainstorming, and use of external management consultants can help to create a short list of strategic options available. Build on your core competencies but also strengthen the gaps and look for alternatives that might help you achieve your performance goals and build on the fundamental strengths of the organization.

Flawlessly Execute

The final step in the strategic planning process is the actual deployment or implementation of the strategies. This is the primary focus of Chapter 10, so we won't cover much here except to say that implementing your strategy is just as important as the strategy itself. Positioning and coordination within your leadership team and board, as well as continuous feedback loops from staff and customers, is necessary to make planning work for you. We call this "performance management" and is the focus of Part III of this book. Implementation typically is comprised of four steps: communicate and ensure internal alignment, obtain feedback about planned strategies, deploy and measure performance, and change or revise direction and strategy as required due to unanticipated events or stakeholder feedback.

Case 4.1: Georgia Community Hospital

Georgia Community Hospital (GCH) is a small, rural hospital in Georgia. With only 120 licensed beds, they are the largest in the region but significantly smaller than the major teaching hospitals in Atlanta and Augusta. The Chief Executive Officer (CEO) recently hired Shelly Hines as Vice President to lead strategic planning and performance improvement. Shelly had worked with several international non-profits and also led planning at a different facility in Mississippi.

Shelly's first task was to organize a planning team and set some guidelines and direction. She asked for a full set of analyses to be conducted, including assessments of the competition and the demographics of their primary customer (patient) base. Her goal was to see if the analyses could point to any specific gaps in the region. The SWOT analysis proved very useful, as the 15-person committee had identified a number of industry opportunities that could be pursued. There were also a lot of weaknesses identified, including quality of staffing and access to specialty physicians. This was the first time that intelligence gathering on the regional competitor hospitals had been conducted in GCH, and it was incredibly useful.

Now, armed with a ton of useful data, Shelly and the CEO are pondering next steps to start formulating useful strategic alternatives for where the organization is headed next.

Planning Tips

Planning is more of an art than a science. Sure, you are using real data to guide you, but how you filter (or process) and interpret them matters more than the evidence itself. Information comes from using analytical tools and techniques, such as market research, competitive intelligence, and scenario models. And it's easy for us to get mired in detail. Here are some practical tips to keep you focused. First, don't let it overwhelm you. Don't let it become too complex, too detailed, or too extensive. Consider the key scenarios and decisions to take. Make those your priority. Second, don't rely solely on a once per year (annual) process for strategic planning. Changes happen too dynamically today, so organizations should toward more real-time and frequent planning processes. Third, don't think about fixed constraints such as budgets. Try to determine what is the absolute best thing to do and then brainstorm how to fund it. Fourth, don't waste time on trying to get complete consensus among the team. That's impossible. Instead, focus your planning on documenting different realms of possibilities. Get them all on the table, and don't leave anything out. Finally, stop thinking of planning as a "must do" or simply an annual exercise. Think about it in terms of a quest or journey toward better strategic thinking. Planning is about considering all available possibilities. Use this time to think through all the opportunities you could exploit.

Strategic planning should be a fun exercise that stretches your imagination as a senior leadership team. If performed correctly, planning can help guide strategic thinking and leadership.

Chapter Summary

- To maintain an effective planning process, leadership is necessary.
- Leaders can help define purpose and vision for the organization, while staff and team members can help provide details around competitors and other intelligence.
- Planning should not be an annual exercise but an ongoing part of strategic leadership.
- Strategic planning should focus on the possibilities and big choices facing your organization.

Discussion Questions

1. What type of strategic planning process does your organization, facility, or department use to set goals and objectives for the future?
2. What is your experience like with planning processes? How can they be improved?
3. Do useful strategies always emerge from the planning process itself? Why or why not?

Key Terms

Market Segment; Risks; Strategic Planning; SWOT Analysis; Threat

References

Langabeer JR, and Napiewocki J (2000). *Competitive Business Strategy for Teaching Hospitals*. Westport, CT: ABC/CLIO and Greenwood Publishing.
Mintzberg H (1994). The rise and fall of strategic planning. *Harvard Business Review*, 4, 107–114.

Chapter 5

Strategic Data Analytics

Erin Donnelly, MHA and Jeff Helton, PhD

Much of contemporary healthcare administration points to ideas such as **evidence-based management**, involving the use of best practices and strategic thinking to identify the best evidence to apply within an organization. Developing strategy and carrying out strategic management calls for the use of evidence to support decisions that shape the ultimate direction of a healthcare business. Successful strategy formulation is grounded in data analytics. This chapter will review the application of data analysis to the formulation, implementation, and monitoring of business strategy in a healthcare organization.

Healthcare strategic planning is a structured process. Once your organization has established its mission, vision, and values, the next step is to understand the business and how it can compete. That competitive analysis should tell the manager what the business does well or what it can do better and how their business stacks up against the competition in the market or perhaps where there are untapped markets for which there may be little or no competition. Typically, this is referred to as the "SWOT analysis", with the acronym standing for strengths, weaknesses, opportunities, and threats (Harrison, 2020; Walston, 2018). The strengths and weaknesses are introspective in nature, looking at what the business does well or could do better. That external look into the competitive market should identify the opportunities for the business or threats to it. To do this sort of analysis well, the organization should leverage its data. This is a particular opportunity for healthcare businesses that tend to have plenty of data but do not use it to inform management decisions (Ladley and Redman, 2020).

DOI: 10.4324/9781032623726-6

From a very broad business perspective, data can create value for the business—not only through informing a thorough SWOT analysis but also through creation of "value modes" for the organization (Ladley and Redman, 2020). These authors describe six value modes that can inform many parts of the traditional SWOT analysis.

Strategic Analytics

Data analytics can yield useful information that can improve internal processes and address an organization's strengths and weaknesses through improved efficiency in executing work or refinement to a customer-facing product such as patient registration, test performance, or billing in a hospital. If those elements are inefficient, then the organization could face lost profitability through wasted resources or customers lost to other competing businesses. So, from a strategic perspective, the organization must deliver work efficiently and of high quality to create an internal strength or avoid an operational weakness.

There can be great value obtained from data that can improve a business' competitive position. Analyzing direct customer feedback from surveys, screening of social media traffic mentioning the business, review of publicly available datasets that describe market share, or financial data from competitors can allow managers to assess how their business compares with others in the market. Such analysis can help the business see potential business opportunities if there appear unmet market needs or product perceptions. It is important to understand that you can use data to identify potential threats to the business, such as loss of market share or comparative disadvantage (e.g., using a financial metric such as cost per unit of output).

Analysis of data from external sources such as social media or market share analysis or customer feedback give managers ideas for new and improved products. Healthcare businesses should be constantly seeking ways to improve products and exploit current product strengths or address weaknesses in those products. Scanning market feedback or market share data could tell managers where opportunities exist to bring new product or service lines to market, such as noting that a competing hospital consistently operates at or near full capacity might suggest that a business could expand their current product offerings to compete against that existing product and capture unmet market demand. Similarly, analysis of financial data may tell managers that their business is able to produce services at a reduced cost and therefore allow for resources to be devoted to service improvement efforts in areas where there may be many sellers in a competitive service line such as obstetrics or outpatient surgery. This sort of analysis can tell managers what market opportunities exist or where a change can be made to exploit a strength.

Data from customer feedback or social media could give managers insight into a form of product improvement known as **informationalization**, where data can be integrated into a product, such as when a hospital adds a patient portal to its website or enables functionality to permit patients to complete registration tasks online. Speeding up a process through informationalization can provide a strategic strength for a business or address a weakness in a situation where the hospital's current registration process creates long waits for service or errors in billing.

Analysis of internal payroll and patient volume data to review labor productivity in different service lines of hospitals could tell managers where labor resources might be misallocated and so identify ways to better utilize scarce human resources. Such an assessment could be viewed as improving human capabilities by finding ways to put employees to a better or more efficient use. That sort of **rightsizing** of staffing within a product line creates a strategic strength or reduces a strategic weakness. That analysis can also create a strategic opportunity if used to create a low-price option in a market or gain market share by creating a price advantage.

Evaluation of market share data or internal financial data can give strategic plans insights usable to manage business risks to the organization. New technologies seem to come to market in health care at a faster and faster pace, requiring potentially sizable financial investments to enter a new strategic market segment with new technologies. However, effective managers use data analytics to evaluate the existing external market and establish a measurable need for that new product before investments are made. Also, analysis of internal operational data can help identify existing capabilities to address that market need or quantify internal resource gaps before investing resources of the business on a decision that could present a significant financial or operational risk.

So using these six value modes described by Ladley and Redman (2020), a case can be made that data can—and should—be the foundation of strategic planning for a healthcare business. The sorts of analyses described earlier in this chapter can in many respects quantify how a strategy can be aligned with the strategic goals of an organization.

Healthcare businesses generate a significant amount of data from routine activities—patient care, payroll, account collections, and purchasing to name a few. This is especially true after passage of the HITECH Act in 2009 which greatly expanded the use of electronic health record technology (Hoyt and Yoshihashi, 2014). In addition, there is a great deal of publicly available data that can help strategic leaders get a better handle on the activities and capabilities of competing businesses (Ning, 2020). Healthcare businesses are increasingly making use of routinely gathered data to evaluate opportunities to improve performance. Analysis of this routinely gathered data for performance improvement is often referred to as analytics (Helton, 2018). Analytics applied to routinely collected business data allows managers to understand operational performance, resource utilization, costs of patient care, and using such information to support managers in making critical decisions about operations (Strome, 2013). Analytics should become the foundation of strategic planning for all businesses but especially those businesses in the healthcare industry with the increased degree of competition, innovation, and reductions in revenues arising from competitive activity.

Analytics for Strategic Planning

Healthcare organizations collect two major types of data—administrative and clinical. Administrative data comes from business-related transactions such as paying invoices or collecting patient accounts. These data elements can help with understanding the costs of operating a healthcare business which can be used to identify potential strengths or weaknesses in how the business is operated. Armed with such intelligence, managers can look for potential areas where the business may want to compete on price against other organizations in the market. This will be advantageous if the organization is adopting a strategy of growth where it will be looking to bring in additional volumes of services. Understanding the operating costs for providing services as well as the available revenues for those services will inform those decisions.

Clinical data comes from documentation created while taking care of patients, including medications, treatments, diagnostic findings, or service usage. These data points can help inform decisions on what the organization does well or perhaps not so well. It can also help identify potential market areas that the business can exploit (Helton, 2018). Examples of administrative and clinical data elements are listed in Table 5.1.

Table 5.1 Examples of Administrative and Clinical Data Elements

Administrative Data	*Clinical Data*
Patient Identification Number	Patient Identification Number
Patient last and first names	Height & weight
Date of birth	Onset of current illness
Home address	Past illness history
Insurance plan data	Blood pressure
Insurance plan contract payment terms	Diagnostic test results
Insurance authorization terms	Medications ordered and administered
Labor hours paid for staff	Procedures performed
Supply purchases	Diagnoses identified

When looking for administrative data to understand the costs of operating a business, decision makers should look to applications such as patient accounting, general ledger accounting, payroll, inventory management, and purchasing (Helton, 2018). Analysis of this business-related data would help the development of a strategic plan by understanding how the business is generating profits, where those profits come from, the expenses involved with providing various services, and where revenues may be improved. All of these types of questions inform the development of the SWOT analysis.

Clinical data that describes the types of services provided to patients comes from applications in the electronic health record, including medication administration, progress notes, medical record abstracts to identify diagnosis and procedure codes used for billing, and use of supply items and diagnostic testing. Data from these sources can tell managers about the most common clinical conditions treated by a healthcare organization so that managers can better understand what markets they participate in, and further evaluation of that data can inform decision makers about the capabilities of the business, what capacity may exist within the business, and also identify areas where the core services of the business are performed well or not so well.

Evaluation of clinical data requires a little more technical expertise than review of administrative data. That is a result of the fact that clinical data comes from licensed healthcare providers such as physicians and nurses. During their work, they will identify illnesses or injuries exhibited by the patient and come up with a diagnosis. Broad groupings of diagnosis can represent service lines for purposes of strategic planning. Examples of such groupings might be diagnosis related with cardiac services or cancer treatment. Those broad areas are considered service lines that may be integrated into a healthcare organization's strategic plan. The clinical applications that provide data on patient diagnoses will allow managers to identify how many patients they see within those service lines and the degree of illness or acuity of those patients. Understanding that acuity will help managers better understand the use of resources in treating patients in those various service lines.

Closely related to understanding the diagnosis treated by an organization is the types of procedures performed within that organization. Procedures include things like surgeries, diagnostic tests, physical examinations, or use of specific medical supplies such as durable medical equipment. Combining procedure data with diagnosis data allows managers to not only understand what types of conditions they are treating within the business but also how they are being treated by caregivers. The combination of these two items can give the managers insight into how it is participating in the local marketplace, and when compared with data from other organizations, how it can help to identify potential opportunities or threats to the business.

Diagnosis data provided from clinical systems is usually captured in the form of a code that is universally accepted for reporting and for billing purposes. That code is known as the ICD 10 code. The ICD acronym stands for International Classification of Diseases, and it is currently being used in its 10th release (hence the "10" suffix behind the acronym). The ICD database is prepared in collaboration with the World Health Organization and is used as the standard manner of describing illnesses and injuries in patients worldwide. Strategic planners can use ICD codes which can be grouped into major diagnostic categories related to body systems in order to identify service lines.

The ICD-10 code set can provide very detailed information about the patients served in the business, even at a much finer level than the broader categories usable to define a service line. ICD-10 codes list a diagnosis, such as myocardial infarction or heart attack. However, these codes can be further elaborated to identify what part of the heart is impacted by coronary disease and allow managers to get a much finer view of what patients are seeking care in the organization but also can identify potential business opportunities if patients are presenting with a condition but are then transferred to another facility. This sort of information comes from the clinical systems available to a healthcare organization manager. Strategic planners can gain a great deal of insight about the markets they serve and potential opportunities through review of simple descriptive statistics reviewing diagnosis codes for a health provider business.

Procedures performed on patients are described using the Common Procedural Terminology or CPT code set. The CPT code set is the property of the American Medical Association and is the commonly accepted method to describe procedures performed on a patient during a healthcare encounter. As noted earlier, CPT codes can be used to identify the types of services being performed on patients and help strategic planners identify potential service lines when used in combination with diagnosis data. Both the ICD-10 and CPT code sets are universally accepted in the US healthcare system for describing diagnostic finding and procedures performed on an invoice for payment by a healthcare provider to an insurer. That invoice is known as a claim. Clinical applications provide the diagnosis and procedure parts of that claim for payment by the provider. Claim data can provide a wealth of actionable information for strategic planning purposes.

Another application of CPT code data for strategic planning purposes comes from evaluation of the organization's performance in current value-based purchasing initiatives used by many insurers in the United States. The CPT code set has specific codes that describe services such as preventive health screenings, patient safety actions, or follow up to earlier diagnostic findings. These codes can be used to identify how often these types of services are provided and to what patients. When tied to data about insurer preventive health measures, managers can get insights on how the organization is meeting value-based purchasing objectives. From a strategic planning perspective, understanding how the organization is doing in these areas could guide decisions on how the organization may undertake strategies to get more involved in population health or value-based payment arrangements. Conversely, analysis of data with these codes can identify potential threats to the business if they are not performing well in areas such as cost per unit of service or in average length of stay for inpatient cases. Strategic planning teams are encouraged to work closely with coding professionals in their health information management department to get an understanding of the diagnosis and procedure codes being used in their organization. In particular, diagnosis codes may require some understanding of basic anatomy and procedure codes may require some understanding of common treatment protocols. Use of clinical resources to understand and interpret this data will greatly assist strategic plan development. Organizations that have a data analytics department may also be able to have resources in that area that will assist strategic planners in evaluating this data for potential business opportunities.

Data from the administrative and clinical applications within a healthcare business are useful for managers to better assess the organization's internal strengths and weaknesses. However, the strategic plan must also include analysis of elements from the external environment in which the organization is operating. There are many useful data sources that can help managers complete an environmental assessment that tells more about potential external threats and business opportunities.

Depending on the type of organization your analysis focuses on, there may be more or fewer data sources that are readily available. External data may be free and publicly available or may require paying a fee or having a subscription. The needs, resources available, and type of organization will determine if the organization can rely on publicly available data or must pay for the data it uses in its strategic planning work.

Large trade organizations like the American Hospital Association ("AHA"), the Medical Group Management Association ("MGMA"), or the American Medical Association ("AMA") have databases available for purchase that can help managers get a good idea of the external competitive landscape by providing a roster of organizations that can be used to determine how competitive a market area is. For example, the AHA database is a listing of AHA members that respond to an annual survey and gathers broad operating statistics and listings of capabilities for hospitals responding to the survey. A similar dataset is available for some physician practices through the MGMA. The AMA has a listing of all practicing physicians with specialties and locations. Health plans can get detailed information on competing insurance providers through a subscription product available from the National Association of Insurance Commissioners ("NAIC"). These databases have some details on the capabilities of competitors but do involve a cost and also may miss some data because of survey responses or an organization not being a member of the organization providing the data. Managers should consider the completeness of data from these sources for the strategic analysis they conduct before making an investment in that data. Strategic analysis data can also come from private data vendors that compile multiple data sources into a convenient set or may even perform specific data queries for a client organization for a fee. A summary of some paid industry organization datasets is provided in Table 5.2.

A limitation of these paid sources is that the data are often collected by qualitative surveys from their members. Certainly, cost may be a limitation

Table 5.2 Examples of Paid Data Sources

Source	Data Available	For More Information
American Hospital Association ("AHA")	Hospital location, operating statistics, capabilities, financial results	https://www.ahadata.com
American Medical Association ("AMA")	Licensed physicians, location, specialty	https://www.ama-assn.org/about/ physician-professional-data/ ama-physician-professional-data
Medical Group Management Association ("MGMA")	Clinic locations, sizes, specialties, operating statistics, financial data	https://www.mgma.com/ mgmadata
National Association of Insurance Commissioners ("NAIC")	Insurer operating statistics, coverages provided, financial results	https://content.naic.org/industry/ insdata

as well if your strategic analysis function is limited in available resources. There are other data sources that are free and publicly available to managers seeking data for an environmental assessment for their businesses. While the data is free, it may require a degree of technical skill to analyze that data as much of it is too voluminous to put into a simple spreadsheet tool like Microsoft Excel. The rudiments of database analysis are beyond the scope of this chapter. Managers that want to perform such analyses are encouraged to develop database skills through a source such as Coursera (www.coursera. org), LinkedIn Learning (www.linkedin.com), or a certificate course from a local college provider.

Many provider facility organizations such as hospitals or nursing homes file financial and operating reports with the federal Centers for Medicare and Medicaid Services ("CMS") and that data is publicly available. CMS is responsible for licensing facility providers. As a part of this licensure process, there are routine site surveys from regulators to gather data on capabilities and operational resources. The CMS Provider of Services file can be a detailed repository for facility operational details such as determining how many organizations in a market area have Magnetic Resonance Imaging (MRI) capabilities or how many nurses they staff in a particular nursing unit. Detailed financial results and operating statistics can be obtained from the annual Medicare Cost Report submitted by facility providers that receive federal funds. The Hospital Cost Report Information System ("HCRIS") database can provide data that can help managers determine market share in general inpatient service lines such as medical/surgical, intensive care unit (ICU), or post-acute care. HCRIS data can also help determine the relative operating costs and revenues for inpatient care and allow managers to determine if other competitors have an advantage in efficiency or if the competition has a weakness that can be exploited.

Since the advent of value-based purchasing as a part of the Patient Protection and Affordable Care Act of 2010, there is much more data available on the clinical performance of healthcare providers through sources such as the Hospital Compare database from CMS. This source tells the public how hospitals are performing on quality of care indicators such as infections or patient safety incidents. Performance scores on patient satisfaction can also be obtained from this source. Managers can analyze this data and get a better idea on how the competition is doing in meeting customer needs and identify areas of potential competitive opportunity or weakness. More information about the various databases available from CMS can be found at https://data.cms.gov.

While data on competitor performance is very useful in a SWOT analysis, additional insights on the broader environment are also needed to provide context for your overall strategic plans. Data on population, demographic characteristics, and community resources are also available in the public domain to better inform strategic planning.

The United States Census Bureau provides data not only about population counts and demographic characteristics such as age and gender distribution within a geographic area but also useful elements on income, insurance coverage, and housing. All of these factors are important in understanding the service area for a healthcare organization. Population counts generated from the decennial census provide a basis for establishing the size of a market area and age/gender breakdowns can help managers establish potential market opportunities based on the demographic profile of a region, such as women's services or senior care options.

The Census Bureau also conducts several community surveys that can be helpful in determining the viability of market opportunities. The American Community Survey data published by the Census Bureau gives additional detail on household size, disposable income, and insurance coverage. Those factors are necessary to understand if potential service lines might be financially viable based on availability of insurance or ability of patients to pay.

Access to this data as well as detailed explanations of the variables available for use can be found at https://data.census.gov.

Further details on access to health insurance coverage is among the resources available from the Agency for Health Research and Quality ("AHRQ"). AHRQ is a central resource for data on health services utilization. Using their Medical Expenditures Panel Survey ("MEPS") data, managers can get data on the costs, utilization patterns, and access to services in their local market. The Healthcare Cost and Utilization Project ("HCUP") dataset gives statistics on inpatient, outpatient, and emergency care encounters as well. These datasets are based on surveys and do not cover every care encounter in a market area. But, the survey methodologies used for these datasets are designed so that the data presents a "best estimate" of market activity and is often used in health services research. So, it can be viewed as reliable for developing analyses of the local healthcare market and assessing potential market opportunities.

As organizations evaluate potential population health strategies, an understanding of social determinants of health ("SDOH") in the market is necessary as the organization assesses opportunities or threats to success. AHRQ publishes databases covering SDOH measures such as poverty or community resources that can inform managers on care gaps that can be filled or areas where a population health strategy may be hindered. In addition to the data from AHRQ, the Centers for Disease Control and Prevention ("CDC") publishes data on the prevalence of chronic conditions, health-related behaviors, and use of preventive health services in its Behavioral Risk Factor Surveillance Survey ("BRFSS") dataset (https://www. cdc.gov/brfss/index.html). More information on AHRQ data resources can be found at https://www.ahrq.gov/data/index.html.

Finally, strategic planners may want to explore a specific disease or condition as a potential business opportunity and need more data on the incidence or prevalence of that condition. CDC publishes data on the prevalence and incidence of disease that can address such planning questions through its BRFSS resources. CDC also publishes vital statistics data on births and deaths with details on live/stillbirths, types of deliveries, or causes of death. Some local Departments of Vital Statistics also publish similar data for their respective service areas. This data is available at a very fine level of geographic detail and can be used for planning at a local community level.

Strategic planning in a healthcare organization should be informed with data and not by anecdote or intuition. The previous section has described a wide array of data sources that can be used in developing a SWOT analysis for a business. But what goes into such an evaluation of the market for strategic planning purposes? The next section will provide some examples of how to perform an external environmental assessment that can help identify potential business opportunities.

Using Data to Perform a Healthcare Environmental Assessment

The use of data is critical to completing an environmental assessment that results in new understandings from which you can draw actionable conclusions. Think of developing an environmental assessment as putting together a jigsaw puzzle. Each element of data you collect on the environment around you is one piece of a very complex puzzle. Collecting these data elements individually is no more useful than having a pile of puzzle pieces on the floor. It's only when you start to put the pieces together do you begin to form a more complete picture of your external environment.

Continuing with this puzzle analogy, it can often be the reality in a strategic planning process that we are unable to gather all of the "pieces". Some external data elements we would like to have are not collected consistently or with high reliability. For example, many states have databases in which most or all hospitals in that state regularly submit hospital admissions at the patient encounter level. This data can be incredibly useful in developing a picture of inpatient market share for each hospital. Patient-level outpatient encounters, however, are often not collected with the same fidelity as inpatient encounters. Certain providers, such as physician-owned surgery or imaging centers, may not have the same reporting requirements as health systems. As such, the outpatient market share "puzzle piece" can often be missing in our environmental assessment. Just because we are missing a puzzle piece does not mean we can't still form a good picture of the environment around us. If we have enough other data elements, we can infer the overall picture through our recognition of patterns, just as you would with a jigsaw puzzle missing a few pieces. In strategic planning analytics, we need to be comfortable with having gaps in our data, gray areas of understanding, and unknowns. Without accepting this reality, we can end up in "analysis paralysis", a state in which you feel you cannot move forward strategically without answering all data questions first.

There are a number of data elements that are typically collected when completing a healthcare environmental assessment. In these elements, we are often looking for both values (such as the population of a particular zip code) and trends (such as whether that population is increasing or decreasing). Data elements commonly used in an environmental assessment include:

- Population
- Use rates
- Market share and competitor analysis
- Insurance coverage and payment models
- Economic outlook
- Governmental regulations/policy
- New technologies/care models
- Healthcare workforce

The data collected should be as specific as possible to the environment in which your organization is operating. For example, knowing the population growth trends of the entire United States, or even for just your state, is not nearly as useful as knowing the population growth trends for the county, city, or zip code in which your hospital or clinic operates. While there are some healthcare services that operate on a national or even international level (i.e. certain telehealth providers, quaternary-level services such as organ transplant), the vast majority of healthcare continues to be sought and provided locally. Depending on the healthcare service type, patients will typically only travel between 10 and 30 minutes for care. And different markets vary greatly. A great strategic tactic in one area of the country might be a terrible idea in another. Therefore, understanding the data elements at a micro-level will result in a much more accurate environmental assessment.

In addition to collecting data that is locally relevant, it is important for the data to be timely. Things change in the environment, sometimes slowly and sometimes at a rapid pace. A new piece of healthcare legislation, such as the Patient Protection and Affordable Care Act of 2010, can result in huge shifts in environmental factors like insurance coverage in a matter of only months or years. An economic downturn can shift population growth projections substantially. A good rule of thumb is that the further back the data element comes from, the less confident we can be in a prediction that is built off of it. For example, population projection tables are regularly reset when the Census is completed every decade. Therefore, population projections built on Census data sourced 3 years ago would likely be more accurate than population projections built on Census data sourced 9 years ago.

The ideal outcome of an environmental assessment is to be able to predict patient demand for a particular service (or set of services) provided by your healthcare institution. Patient demand can be expressed numerically in terms of patient volumes. If you know, or can predict, the patient volumes for a service, you can appropriately "right size" your service offerings to make them financially viable, while also being competitive. Accurately predicting patient volumes allows hospital administrators to plan for the correct number of physical assets (i.e. patient rooms, operating rooms, clinic rooms, emergency department bays, imaging machines) and workforce (i.e. physicians, nurses, therapists, support staff) to make an operation run smoothly.

Calculating patient demand is a mathematical equation consisting of three of the environmental assessment data elements mentioned above: Population, use rate, and market share.

If you know the population of people that could use a healthcare service ("population"), you can multiply this by the number of people per 1,000 that actually do use this service ("use rate") to get the total number of patient volumes expected from that group of people. Figure 5.1 shows the patient demand calculation.

If a health system then knows the percentage of these patients who will likely seek care at their institution rather than that of a competitor ("market share"), they can appropriately plan for these patient volumes through this calculation:

Total Market Volumes × Est. Market Share = Expected Patient Volumes

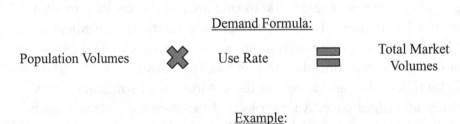

Demand Formula:

Population Volumes ✖ Use Rate ＝ Total Market Volumes

Example:

Pop. Volume Estimate	Use Rate	Total Market Volume
Number of women ages 15-44	Births per 1,000 women ages 15-44	Projected Births
10,000	6.3 per 1,000	563 births

Figure 5.1   Calculating patient demand.

For example, if projected births were 563, and the market share of that facility was 25%, then the estimated demand or number of births at your facility would be 141 deliveries.

Because this same mathematical equation is useful in all types of healthcare strategic planning circumstances, we gather the other common environmental assessment data elements listed above for the purposes of understanding how these numerically impact the values and/or trends of the three key areas of population, use rate, and market share. Examples of these data elements are listed in Table 5.3.

Table 5.3   Examples of Common Data Analysis Elements

Data Element	Examples of Impact on Population	Examples of Impact on Use Rate	Examples of Impact on Market Share
Insurance Coverage		Uninsured individuals use healthcare services at a substantially lower rate than those who are commercially insured. Medicare-insured individuals use many healthcare services at a higher rate than those commercially insured.	Certain healthcare institutions are contracted with specific commercial insurance carriers. A change in insurance carrier for a large population (such as a union or major employer) can shift market share between delivery organizations.
Economic Outlook	When the economy is more favorable in a geographic area, the birth rate and immigration may increase.	When the economy is less favorable, people with high-deductible health plans put off seeking elective care.	

(Continued)

Table 5.3 (*Continued*) Examples of Common Data Analysis Elements

Data Element	Examples of Impact on Population	Examples of Impact on Use Rate	Examples of Impact on Market Share
Governmental Regulations/ Policy	Tax rebates for childcare may encourage families to have more children. Tax incentives may encourage major employers to move to a new area.	Governmental payers such as Medicare or Medicaid may change the "site of service" they will pay for certain procedures, shifting those services from inpatient to outpatient.	A Certificate of Need (CON) program may limit the number of competitors that can enter a market and how quickly each entity can grow.
New Technologies/ Care Models	New vaccines may result in higher survival rates of a once vulnerable population.	A new technology may allow for an alternative outpatient procedure that reduces hospitalizations compared to the prior inpatient care model.	A superior technology offered only at a single organization may result in market share shifting between competitors.
Healthcare Workforce		Gaps in workforce may lead to delays in care, resulting in patients not being provided services they sought.	Specialized providers only available at one competitor may increase their market share in a specific program over another competitor.

In order to better understand the three key data elements in a healthcare environmental assessment, we will now discuss each individually.

Population

Population is, simply put, a number of people. Census data is considered the "gold standard" for population numbers, but because this is updated fully only once a decade, timeliness of Census data can pose a problem. Most states provide updated population data elements to the public, such as births and deaths, through the Department of Vital Statistics or the Census Bureau. Many states also perform their own population projections on a regular basis for use in research and planning. It is important to recognize that population numbers can vary quite a bit between these different data sources. Some can have more conservative growth projections, while others may view population growth from a bullish perspective. It is important to stay consistent with the data source of your choice throughout a strategic planning project, so accurate comparisons can be made between different strategic opportunities.

The population you choose to use will depend on the area(s) of interest for your environmental assessment. Sometimes, the entire population of a geography is appropriate. Often, however, a refined population is more helpful. For example, you may want to limit your population numbers by age if you are performing an environmental assessment on pediatric services. A geographic area can have a very different growth rate in child vs. adult populations, so narrowing to a population of only ages 0–18, and using their specific attributed growth rate, will make your analysis more accurate. You would want to limit your population by male or female for sex-linked conditions such as prostate cancer or pregnancy. You may want to limit a population by race or ethnicity, if you are evaluating a programmatic opportunity for a health condition that disproportionately impacts a particular community, such as sickle cell anemia or Tay-Sachs disease. Limiting population by a payer group, such as Medicare enrollees, is commonly used because there can be such a difference in use rates for older patients than the population at large.

Populations can grow or decline due to a number of factors. Births lead to population growth; so does immigration. Deaths lead to population decline, as does people moving out of the area. Aging does not have an impact on overall population numbers, but aging can affect numbers of subpopulations you may want to use, such as the number of children or Medicare enrollees. Once you have selected a population to use, and determined an appropriate rate of growth or decline, next you'll want to determine a use rate.

Use Rate

Use rate is the use of a specific healthcare service per a defined population. Use rate is typically expressed in "patients per 1,000 population", though this denominator can vary depending on the frequency of encounters. Some examples of use rates include:

- Inpatient encounters per 1,000 people in Colorado
- Births per 1,000 women aged 18–44
- Hip replacements per 10,000 Medicare enrollees
- Vaccinations received per 1,000 students
- Chemotherapy treatments per person living with breast cancer
- Notice the clearly defined healthcare service and clearly defined population for each.

When talking about use rates, it is important to distinguish between the terms prevalence and incidence. Prevalence is the number of total cases in a population at one time. Incidence is the number of new cases in a population during a specific time period. Sometimes, one is better to use than another in a strategic assessment. For example, a cancer patient uses different healthcare services in their first year of diagnosis (incidence) than they do in years of ongoing maintenance care (prevalence). For cancer surgery, you may want to use the incidence rate, but for chemotherapy, the prevalence rate may be more appropriate. Knowing which to use helps you better predict patient volumes.

Just like populations, use rates can grow or decline over time. Some examples of environmental factors that can cause use rates to grow or decline in a population include:

- Changes in incidence or prevalence of disease
- Changes in treatment protocols
- Site-of-service changes (such as inpatient moving to outpatient) driven by payers
- Changes in patient behavior or preferences

Once you have landed on how you expect the use rate to change over time, you have enough information to calculate expected total market volumes.

Market Share

Market share is the proportion of customer volumes that will be coming to your organization, as opposed to that of a competitor. Market share is typically displayed as a percentage of a defined market total. The market total (all the possible patients/customers/members) is calculated using the population and use rate numbers determined previously.

Sometimes, you will have actual market share information at your disposal. As mentioned previously, most states regularly collect inpatient admissions data from hospitals within the state. You can limit this data by the population you have selected for your environmental assessment (by age, sex, zip code, health condition) and then see which hospital each patent went to for care. The sum of all of the patients in this population who received care at your hospital divided by the sum of all of the possible patients within this defined population will yield the market share percentage.

141 births at country hospital ÷ 563 total market birth = 25% market share

Sometimes, market share will need to be inferred. When total market volume data is unavailable, as is the case for many outpatient services, there are a few ways market share can be estimated. First, if you know the population of patients likely to use a service, and you have researched the use rate of a healthcare service for that population, you can estimate total market volumes. If you know your internal volumes at your hospital for this service, you can divide that number into the estimated total market volumes to get a market share approximation. Alternatively, if you know your hospital's market share for a related inpatient service, you can use this as an approximation for outpatient market share as well. For example, perhaps you don't know your market share for outpatient orthopedic surgeries. But you do have access to your market share for inpatient orthopedic surgeries. Although there would be caveats to using inpatient market share as an approximation for outpatient market share for the same service line, it is perhaps a good place to start. It is important to realize, however, when using an estimate for market share as your starting point, you have a larger margin of error for your future projections. This is a case in which scenario planning, in which you might try multiple market share percentages (i.e. 10%, 15%, and 20%) to see how different your projections become, can help you to better understand the financial impact that could arise from errors related to estimations in market share.

When trying to project future market share for a healthcare service, understanding market structure will provide significant insight into your current and future competitive positions. Market structure is defined by the number of competitors and the likelihood of new market entrants.

Detailed description of varied market structures is beyond the scope of this chapter, but understanding the broad categories of market will help with interpreting the results of a market analysis. Markets where there is one provider of a good or service is a monopoly. It is important to note that in healthcare, rarely is there a pure monopoly where one institution has 100% market share. Even in markets with only a single hospital or unique program, patients can travel to other locations for that care (Henderson, 2018).

Markets where there are a larger number of competitors—enough so that one seller does not control the market—are competitive markets. In most markets, there is neither a monopoly nor a purely competitive structure. Because of the barriers to entry in health care (e.g., cost, licensure), the extent of competition in a market area relates as much to the number of available customers (population) and the resources available to pay for care (insurance).

Case 5.1: Metropolitan Medical Center

Lauren James was just appointed to the newly created position of Chief Strategy Officer of Metropolitan Medical Center. During the interview process, several board members and the CEO commented that Metropolitan had "most of the market share for inpatients in the service area". She was concerned about this perception as her prior employer, University Hospital had been making similar assertions while she worked there. Lauren wanted to put some data behind those conflicting positions and start her new position with a data-informed idea of market shares in the community.

Lauren's data analyst, Cody was immediately tasked with getting that objective market share information to inform future discussions about market share at Metropolitan. Cody had just finished a short course on health data analysis at the local university. He had just reviewed the Medicare Cost Report Data he had downloaded from the CMS website and saw that one worksheet in the cost report was devoted solely to patient day and discharge data for hospitals. Lauren and Cody knew this would be a quick "win" for the strategic planning function.

Using a list of all seven hospitals in the Metropolitan service area, Cody was able to create a quick listing of inpatient discharges showing that University Hospital had 37% of the inpatient services market, while Metropolitan was second highest with 28% of the local inpatient market. Lauren now had data to support her arguments for new service expansions to grow market share.

Using Data to Perform an Internal Assessment

Once you have completed your environmental assessment, the next step is to complete an internal assessment. Your mission, vision, and values define who you are as an organization and who you strive to be. The environmental assessment you perform tells you what is going on in the world around you. Your internal assessment is an evaluation of how you are prepared to respond to what is going on in the world around you, in light of who you are and who you are striving to be.

Performing an honest internal assessment requires the gathering of multiple internal data sources, different than those external sources used in your environmental assessment. You'll be wanting to consider your organization's strengths and weaknesses from many different vantage points. Some examples of the variety of data to gather in an internal assessment are shown in Table 5.4.

Table 5.4 Examples of Internal Assessment Analyses

Organizational Attributes	Examples of Questions to Be Asked/Data to Be Collected
Operational Efficiency	What is our current customer wait times? How often do we have "downtimes" in our operations today? How many resources (rooms, pieces of equipment) do we have today? What is the current throughput of these resources? Are we maximizing the use of our current assets, or do we have capacity to do more?
Customer Satisfaction	What is the community perception of our organization? What are our current patient satisfaction scores? What are the major drivers of customer satisfaction or dissatisfaction?
Workforce Readiness	How many providers do we have today for these services? Would we need to add providers to expand services? If so, how many and what types? How satisfied are current providers with the type of work they are performing and their workload?
Financial Performance	How financially sustainable are the services we offer today? Which services are profitable, and which are unprofitable? Will adding patient volumes increase or decrease profitability?

Just like with the environmental assessment, these data elements need to not just be gathered but also analyzed in a way that illuminates actions to be taken. Your environmental assessment will present you with market opportunities, such as:

■ A 5% growth in market share for cancer services would result in an additional 350 inpatients per year.
■ Population growth is going to result in 1,200 additional births at our hospitals over the next decade.
■ Use rate changes will shift 600 inpatient surgeries to outpatient procedures in the next 3 years.

Your internal assessment will help you determine (1) if you are prepared to capture these market opportunities, and (2) if these market opportunities make sense (financially, operationally, culturally) for your institution to go after. We always have constrained resources and strategic planning is about prioritization. Just because a market opportunity exists, this doesn't mean our organization is the right one to pursue it.

We can best explain how the data from your internal assessment complements the data from your environmental assessment with an example. Let's say after performing an environmental assessment, you determine there is significant market opportunity to grow your oncology infusion services for chemotherapy treatment. You estimate that you can capture 10% additional market share, resulting in 1,500 more infusion treatments per year. In your internal assessment, you'll want to look at data to answer the following questions:

■ *Operational Efficiency*: How many cancer infusion rooms/chairs do we have today? How many treatments per chair are being completed per week? How many treatments per chair could be completed per week if we were operating at maximum capacity? Do we have the capacity within our current assets to accommodate an additional 1,500 treatments per year? If not, how many additional assets would we need to add?
■ *Customer Satisfaction*: What is the community's current view of our cancer services? Are we a top performer in patient satisfaction? Which elements of patient satisfaction need to be improved to capture more market share?

■ *Workforce Readiness*: How many medical oncologists do we have today? What is their current patient load per provider? How many infusion nurses do we have today? What is our workforce turnover rate? What is our workforce satisfaction in oncology services? Do we have capacity within our current providers to accommodate another 1,500 treatments per year? Or would we need to add more providers, and if so, how many?

■ *Financial Performance*: Is chemotherapy currently a financially profitable service? If so, what is the profitability per incremental patient? Does profitability increase or decrease with additional patient volume? Would profitability increase or decrease if we need to add assets (rooms, providers) to accommodate 1,500 new treatments per year?

When we ask questions about capacity, as those proposed above, we are trying to determine if we have the right resources in place to accommodate strategic growth. Sometimes, we don't know what our optimal capacity is. For example, we might typically do ten operations per day per operating room. But how do we know if we have the capacity to do 12 operations per room per day instead? This is a situation in which benchmarking can come in handy. Benchmarking is comparing your internal metrics to those of "like organizations" to see how you perform in comparison. Good benchmarking tools are available from a variety of affinity organizations and consulting firms. The most important part of benchmarking is to determine the similarities and differences between the organizations being compared. Continuing with our operating room example, a benchmarking effort might reveal that ten surgeries per operating room per day puts our throughput at the 45th percentile of all hospitals reporting to the benchmarking organization. At the 95th percentile, hospitals actually accommodate 16 surgeries per day per operating room. This does not necessarily mean we have the capacity to add six surgeries to each OR per day. Perhaps the hospitals at the 95th percentile accommodate much shorter procedures than our hospital. Or perhaps those hospitals do not need to leave OR space open for trauma surgeries that could unexpectedly arrive through our emergency department. Benchmarks are a useful tool to understand what might be possible, in all sorts of internal metrics from throughput to patient satisfaction to financial performance, but they require deeper analysis to determine realistic goals for your own institution.

Chapter Summary

- Data can be used to improve internal and external analyses.
- Careful understanding of how to use these data points to calculate demand, market share, and forecasts will help improve strategic planning considerably.
- Multiple data sources and organizations exist to provide useful comparison from other organizations, including your competitors.

Discussion Questions

1. What data elements does your organization currently utilize on a regular basis for planning purposes?
2. Which metrics, and therefore data, are most useful to your organization today (workforce efficiency, financials, customer satisfaction)? Do all data from these sources get stored in a central database?
3. What evidence-based practices does your organization utilize?

Key Terms

Evidence-Based Management; Informationalization; Rightsizing; SWOT

References

Harrison J (2020). *Essentials of Strategic Planning in Healthcare* (3rd ed). Chicago, IL: Health Administration Press.

Helton J (2018). Health Care Analytics, Chapter 8. In Langabeer, J. (Ed.) *Performance Improvement in Hospitals and Health Systems* (2nd ed). Burlington, MA: Taylor & Francis.

Henderson J (2018). *Health Economics and Policy* (7th ed). Boston, FL: Cengage.

Hoyt R and Yoshihashi A (2014). *Health Informatics: Practical Guide for Healthcare and Information Technology Professionals* (6th ed). Pensacola, FL: Informatics Education.

Ladley J and Redman T (2020). Use data to accelerate your business strategy. *Harvard Business Review*, March 3, 2020.

Ning X (2020). Operations-Intelligence-Strategy (OIS) in Healthcare, Chapter 4, p.88. In Khuntia, J., Ning, X., and Tanniru, M. (Ed.) *Theory and Practice of Business Intelligence in Healthcare*. Hershey, PA: IGI Global.

Strome T (2013). *Healthcare Analytics for Quality and Performance Improvement*. Hoboken, NJ: Wiley.

Walston S (2018). *Strategic Healthcare Management: Planning and Execution* (2nd ed). Chicago, IL: Health Administration Press.

STRATEGIC LEADERSHIP

Chapter 6

Leadership

Karima Lalani, PhD

An Evolution in Leadership

The healthcare industry continues to evolve at a rapid pace, and healthcare entities require leaders to guide, influence, and manage the various aspects of organizations and systems effectively. The industry is continuing to transform in order to navigate the post-COVID landscape, and strong and effective leadership skills will continue to play a crucial role as organizations adapt to the post-pandemic realities.

So, why is healthcare leadership important? Effective healthcare leadership is essential for ensuring the safety and well-being of patients. Leaders set the tone for patient-centered care and are imperative in promoting a culture of safety within healthcare organizations. Healthcare leaders also play a crucial role in implementing and monitoring quality improvement initiatives—they are responsible for establishing and maintaining high standards of care, which can lead to better patient outcomes.

Healthcare leaders are also tasked with developing and implementing strategic plans that address the ever-changing healthcare landscape, including advancements in medical technology, evolving regulations, as well as shifting demographics. They engage in policy advocacy at both the organizational and industry levels and work to shape healthcare policies that benefit patients and their organizations. Community engagement is also essential for healthcare leaders, as they must engage with the community and build trust and must ensure that the services are accessible to their community's needs.

DOI: 10.4324/9781032623726-8

The healthcare industry is also faced with a variety of significant financial challenges (Lalani et al., 2021), and healthcare leaders must also possess financial acumen for managing budgets, controlling costs, and ensuring the long-term financial sustainability of their organizations. The healthcare spending in the United States continues to increase, in comparison with other developed nations, and in 2016, the United States spent nearly 18% of its gross domestic product (GDP) on healthcare (Lalani et al., 2021). Additionally, the ability to be agile and adopt to the ever-changing technological landscape within the industry is also essential for healthcare leaders, so that new technologies and platforms can be integrated into the service delivery.

Leadership Styles

Leadership in healthcare can take various forms, and different leadership styles are suited to different healthcare settings and situations. **Leadership style** refers to the leader's system of providing overarching direction, planning, deciding, and motivating employees within an organization. We think of leadership as the purview of only management of an organization, but leadership can also be exhibited both formally and informally within an organization. Some common leadership styles found in healthcare organizations are listed below. Which of these types do you identify with the most?

■ *Transformational Leadership*: Transformational leaders inspire and motivate their teams to achieve higher levels of performance and innovation (Avolio et al., 2009). They often foster a culture of continuous improvement and can adapt well to rapidly changing healthcare environments. Transformational leadership can be well-suited to academic medical centers, research institutions, and healthcare organizations focused on innovation and quality improvement.

■ *Servant Leadership*: Defined as a philosophy and set of practices that enrich the lives of individuals and build organizations, servant leadership emphasizes increasing service to others, a holistic approach to work, and promoting a sense of community (Spears, 1996). Servant leaders prioritize the well-being of their team members and patients above all else. They foster a culture of empathy, collaboration, and patient-centered care. This approach can lead to high levels of employee satisfaction and patient outcomes. Servant leadership is well-suited to healthcare settings where patient satisfaction and team well-being are top priorities, such as hospice care or long-term care facilities.

- *Transactional Leadership*: Transactional leaders are skilled at setting clear expectations, providing rewards for performance (Avolio et al., 2009), and addressing problems as they arise. They are effective at maintaining order and compliance within healthcare teams. This style may stifle creativity and innovation since it primarily relies on established protocols and procedures. Transactional leadership can be effective in large, established healthcare organizations where adherence to established standards and procedures is crucial, such as in government-run healthcare facilities.

- *Democratic Leadership*: Democratic leaders involve team members in decision-making, which can lead to innovative solutions and high levels of team buy-in. This approach can also foster a collaborative and inclusive culture (Ronald, 2014). It may be time-consuming, and consensus-building can be challenging, especially in urgent situations where quick decisions are needed. Democratic leadership can be effective in healthcare organizations that value collaboration, such as community health clinics and interdisciplinary care teams.

In reality, healthcare leadership often requires a blend of these styles, adapted to specific situations and the needs of the team and patients. Leaders in healthcare should be flexible and able to adjust their leadership style as circumstances change. Moreover, a successful leader may employ different styles in different aspects of their role, as necessitated by their organization and circumstances. This refers to the **strategic fit**, which is alignment of leadership style with the individual's personality and characteristics, as well as the organization's needs and environment. Different situations call for different leadership styles. In times of financial turnarounds, organizations might call for more controlling, cost-focused leadership styles. While in growing and innovative organizations, it might be more transformational.

Qualities of Good Healthcare Leaders

Effective healthcare leaders also play a crucial role in shaping the quality of patient care, the culture of their organizations, and the overall success of healthcare institutions. To excel in this role, healthcare leaders should possess a wide range of qualities and skills. Some examples of these qualities include:

- *Empathy*: Healthcare leaders must be empathetic, able to understand and connect with patients, their families, and their colleagues. Empathy helps leaders make decisions that prioritize the well-being and satisfaction of patients and foster a positive and supportive work environment for staff (Moudatsou et al., 2020).
- *Empowering*: Leaders have to empower their managers and staff to carry out plans and actions that are aligned with the strategic direction of the organization.
- *Communication Skills*: Clear and effective communication is paramount in healthcare leadership. Leaders should be able to convey information clearly to diverse audiences, including patients, staff, and other stakeholders (Johns, 2017). They must also be skilled listeners to understand the concerns and feedback of others.
- *Adaptability*: The healthcare landscape is constantly evolving due to advances in medical technology, changes in healthcare policy, and shifts in patient needs. Leaders need to be adaptable and open to change, willing to embrace new approaches and technologies to improve patient care and organizational performance.
- *Patient-Centered Approach*: Healthcare leaders should have an unwavering commitment to patient-centered care. This means putting the patient's needs, preferences, and values at the center of all healthcare decisions. Leaders should also advocate for patient rights and work to create a culture of patient-centeredness within their organizations.
- *Ethical Integrity*: Healthcare leaders must exhibit strong ethical integrity. They should make decisions that prioritize the best interests of patients and adhere to ethical principles even when facing challenging situations (Johns, 2017). Upholding ethical standards is essential for maintaining trust within the healthcare system.
- *Strategic Thinking*: Effective healthcare leaders are strategic thinkers who can set a clear vision for their organizations, develop strategic plans, and execute initiatives to achieve long-term goals (Ginter et al., 2018). They should be able to analyze data, anticipate trends, and make informed decisions that drive organizational success.
- *Team Building and Collaboration*: Building and leading effective healthcare teams is crucial. Leaders should be skilled in recruiting, developing, and motivating staff. They should also encourage collaboration

among different departments and professions to improve patient outcomes.

■ *Problem-Solving Skills*: Healthcare leaders encounter complex challenges regularly. They must be adept at problem-solving and decision-making, using data and evidence-based practices to address issues and improve processes (Ginter et al., 2018).

■ *Resilience*: The healthcare industry can be emotionally and mentally demanding. Leaders should have the resilience to cope with stress and adversity while maintaining their focus on patient care and organizational goals. They should also provide support and resources to help their teams build resilience.

■ *Cultural Competency*: In today's diverse healthcare environment, leaders should be culturally competent, respecting and valuing the diverse backgrounds and beliefs of patients and staff. This promotes inclusivity and equity in healthcare delivery.

Case 6.1: Eastside Hospital CEO

Dr. Jane Benoit, a seasoned physician, found herself at a crossroads when she was appointed as the new Chief Executive Officer of Eastside Community Hospital. The community hospital had been struggling with financial instability as well as declining patient satisfaction scores. The former CEO was a transactional-based leader and had not made significant investments in capital or human resources during his tenure, and for that reason, the hospital was suffering. Dr. Benoit was known for her clinical expertise, community engagement, and patient-centered approach from a neighboring facility. Her first task was prioritizing collaboration and transparency in all decisions. She started engaging the hospital staff in the annual budgeting process, capital investment committees, and focused on fostering a culture of continuous improvement. She also started a Six Sigma project for the two largest service lines, obstetrics and surgery. Over time, Eastside Community Hospital not only regained financial stability but also earned a reputation as a model of patient-centric care, due to Dr. Benoit's transformational healthcare leadership.

This case study illustrates Dr. Benoit's leadership journey, showcasing the critical role of visionary leadership in revitalizing a struggling healthcare institution and redefining its place in the community. It also highlights the importance of balancing clinical and administrative expertise, and the profound impact of fostering a culture of collaboration and continuous improvement in healthcare settings.

Importance of Leadership Development in Healthcare

Leadership development programs and continuous learning are of paramount importance for healthcare professionals due to their multifaceted role in delivering quality patient care, managing healthcare organizations, and driving innovation in an ever-evolving industry. Effective leadership ensures that healthcare professionals make informed decisions, prioritize patient safety, and provide the best possible care (Ginter et al., 2018). Well-trained leaders can lead healthcare teams to coordinate care seamlessly, reducing medical errors and improving patient outcomes.

The healthcare industry is dynamic, with constant advancements in technology, treatment modalities, and regulatory changes. Continuous learning equips healthcare professionals with the skills and knowledge needed to adapt to these changes and remain at the forefront of their field. Healthcare is a team-based endeavor, and leadership development programs foster collaboration and effective communication among professionals. Strong leaders can create cohesive, high-performing teams that work harmoniously to achieve common goals.

Leaders often drive innovation and research within healthcare organizations. Continuous learning encourages healthcare professionals to explore new ideas, technologies, and approaches to patient care, which can lead to groundbreaking discoveries and improved treatments. Leadership development equips healthcare professionals with the skills to manage resources efficiently, make strategic decisions, and optimize healthcare delivery. This is crucial for the financial sustainability of healthcare organizations.

Healthcare organizations should establish formal leadership development programs that identify and nurture leadership potential from within their ranks. These programs may include mentorship, training, and experiential learning opportunities (Johns, 2017). Organizations should also encourage healthcare professionals to pursue advanced degrees, certifications, and specialized training. Offering incentives or study leave can motivate individuals to invest in their own development.

Pairing aspiring leaders with experienced mentors or coaches who can provide guidance, share their experiences, and offer constructive feedback can also aid in leadership development. Encouraging healthcare professionals to gain experience in different departments or roles within the organization, as well as exposure to various aspects of healthcare operations, can broaden their perspectives and skill sets. Organizing workshops, seminars, and conferences focused on leadership and management in healthcare can also provide networking opportunities and expose professionals to best practices.

Challenges Faced by Healthcare Leaders

Healthcare leaders face a myriad of unique challenges due to the dynamic nature of the healthcare industry. Three significant challenges they encounter include the constant evolution of medical technology, regulatory changes, and the increasing demand for cost-effective care. Here's an overview of each challenge and the role of healthcare leaders in addressing them:

- *Continual Evolution of Medical Technology*: The rapid pace of medical technology advancements presents both opportunities and challenges for healthcare leaders. New technologies can improve patient outcomes, enhance diagnostics, and streamline operations, but they also require significant investments and ongoing training for staff. Leaders in healthcare organizations must stay abreast of emerging technologies and assess their potential impact. They need to make informed decisions regarding technology adoption, ensuring that new tools align with the organization's strategic goals. Additionally, they should promote a culture of innovation and continuous learning within their teams to harness the benefits of technology effectively.
- *Regulatory Changes*: The healthcare industry in the United States is highly regulated, and regulations can change frequently at both the federal and state levels. These changes can affect reimbursement models, quality standards, data privacy, and more. Staying compliant with evolving regulations is essential to avoid penalties and maintain patient trust. Healthcare leaders must establish strong compliance and risk management processes within their organizations. They should closely monitor regulatory developments and adapt policies and procedures accordingly. Effective communication within the organization is vital to ensure that all staff members are aware of and can adhere to changing regulations. Leaders should also advocate for industry-wide collaboration to shape favorable policies and regulations.
- *Increasing Demand for Cost-Effective Care*: Healthcare costs continue to rise, putting pressure on organizations to deliver high-quality care while controlling expenses (Lalani et al., 2021). Balancing the need for cost-effective care with maintaining quality and patient satisfaction is an ongoing challenge. Healthcare leaders play a crucial role in driving cost-effective care by implementing efficient processes, optimizing resource allocation, and adopting value-based care models. They should encourage and foster a culture of innovative approaches to care delivery and payment models. Collaboration with payers, providers,

and patients is essential to achieve cost-effective outcomes, while maintaining quality.

■ *Fostering a Culture of Innovation*: Leaders should create an environment where staff members are encouraged to explore and implement innovative ideas. This involves providing resources, support, and recognition for innovative efforts. Allocating resources for research and development allows healthcare organizations to develop and test new approaches to care, treatments, and technologies.

■ *Collaborating with External Partners*: Healthcare leaders should seek partnerships with startups, academic institutions, and technology companies to leverage external expertise and stay at the forefront of innovation.

■ *Data-Driven Decision-Making*: Leveraging data analytics and insights can help leaders identify areas for improvement and innovation, whether it's in patient care, operational efficiency, or resource allocation.

Driving Innovation

Healthcare leaders play a crucial role in driving innovation and managing change within the healthcare sector. Their responsibilities extend beyond just overseeing day-to-day operations; they must also lead their organizations in adapting to an ever-evolving healthcare landscape. As the industry continues to become more complex, healthcare leaders must establish a clear vision for innovation within their organizations. This vision should align with the organization's mission and values while also embracing technological advancements and new care models.

Effective leaders need to continue to foster a culture where innovation is encouraged and employees feel empowered to propose and implement new ideas. They need to prioritize a culture that values continuous learning, experimentation, and improvement. Healthcare leaders also need to strike a balance in the realm of resource allocation, to ensure that not only current services are maintained and provided but also investments in future-oriented projects are also pursued. Innovation often involves taking calculated risks, and leaders must assess and manage these risks, recognizing that not all innovative efforts will succeed, but some may yield significant benefits.

Leadership in healthcare is pivotal for delivering high-quality patient care, improving organizational performance, and navigating the dynamic healthcare industry. Effective healthcare leaders must adapt to changing circumstances, embrace innovation, and prioritize patient-centric care while addressing the evolving challenges in healthcare. Healthcare is a multidisciplinary field, and leaders must facilitate collaboration among various stakeholders, including physicians, nurses, researchers, and administrators. Visionary leaders with the agility and the ability to adopt to the ever-evolving landscape of the healthcare industry will be essential to steer the healthcare organizations successfully and work toward improving health of the populations they serve.

Chapter Summary

- The most dominant leadership styles are transformational, servant leader, transactional, and democratic, although there are numerous other less common styles.
- The most effective leadership styles are those that are strategically aligned with the organization and with the individual's own characteristics. There is no one "best" or optimal leadership style for all organizations. The style needs to fit the environment and the strategy. This represents the concept of strategic fit.
- The essential characteristics of most effective leaders typically include empathy, communication, team building, and many more. While nobody can have all of them, it is important that healthcare executives embrace what they can and work on developing in the areas they lack.
- Some of the most recent challenges faced by healthcare executives include the growth in medical and information technology, increased regulations, higher focus on cost-effective care, and increased need to strategically coordinate with outside partners and players.

Discussion Questions

1. You have likely seen, or will see, multiple types of managers during your career. Which type of leadership style do you think you could work best for?
2. If a hospital is suffering extreme financial losses, is there one specific style you would suggest senior leadership adopt?
3. What other challenges do you see facing healthcare leaders for the future?

Key Terms

Strategic Fit; Leadership Style

References

Avolio BJ, Walumbwa FO, and Weber TJ (2009). Leadership: current theories, research, and future directions. *Annual Review of Psychology*, *60*(1), 421–449. https://doi.org/10.1146/annurev.psych.60.110707.163621

Ginter PM, Duncan WJ, and Swayne LE (2018). *Strategic Management of Health Care Organizations*. Hoboken, NJ: John Wiley & Sons, Inc.

Johns ML (2017). *Leadership Development for Healthcare: A Pathway, Process, and Workbook*. Chicago, IL: American Health Information Management Association.

Lalani K, Revere L, Chan W, Champagne-Langabeer T, Tektiridis J, and Langabeer J (2021). Impact of external environmental dimensions on financial performance of major organizations in the U.S. *Healthcare*, *9*(8), 1069. https://doi.org/10.3390/healthcare9081069

Moudatsou M, Stavropoulou A, Philalithis A, and Koukouli S (2020). The role of empathy in health and social care professionals. *Healthcare*, *8*(1), 26. https://doi.org/10.3390/healthcare8010026

Ronald B (2014). Comprehensive leadership review: literature, theories and research. *Advances in Management*, 7(5), 52–66.

Spears L (1996). Reflections on Robert K. greenleaf and servant leadership. *Leadership and Organization Development Journal*, *17*(7), 33–35.

Chapter 7

Leaders as Entrepreneurs

How Leaders Choose

Organizations and consumers alike routinely make selections between alternatives or choices. These choices could propel an organization to buy a new building or start a new service line. As consumers, we choose how much to spend and where to live. Decisions are all around us daily. The pattern of choices over time, both high-magnitude and resource-intensive (strategic) and small (routine, day-to-day), will make or break companies and consumers. This is complicated since, as humans, we are often ruled by less than rational thought. Our actions are tightly coupled with hidden emotions, thoughts, and feelings so concepts of behavioral economics are especially insightful. Behavioral economics involves assessing how human behavior impacts economic decision-making. This is especially difficult when large organizations, with thousands of employees, are involved.

Theories involving the experience curve suggest that the more we do of something, the better we get. We learn how to do certain things better, and we get faster and more efficient. But despite what people might think, this doesn't happen with most decision-making. We don't see evidence of large-scale learning and improvement in choices simply based on experience. It's much more than that.

Although we make hundreds of choices routinely, we make most of them at the subconscious level using a combination of heuristics, habits, and hunches. **Heuristics** are mental shortcuts that reduce the burden on our mind,

DOI: 10.4324/9781032623726-9

while a **habit** is a behavior that is so ingrained that it requires almost no conscious thought. **Hunches**, or intuition, are our gut-level instincts. All three can be helpful to speed up the decision process, but they can also be detrimental to a decision's quality and outcomes. They tend to result in biases, such as overconfidence or possibly risk aversion. When we rely on these exclusively, our judgment is limited and we make less than stellar choices.

When we examine the decision process of managers and leaders, we find similar patterns. We tend to shortcut in one of three areas: (1) either we don't fully recognize the magnitude of the consequences for the decision at the time we make it; (2) we aren't fully aware of all available alternatives; or (3) we didn't spend adequate time contemplating the choice.

Leadership has an especially challenging task when managing hundreds or thousands of employees. The idea of **behavioral congruence**, which is the alignment of our analytical reasoning with our intuitive and emotional processing, requires us to be much more present and aware of consequences of our decisions. Strategic decision, those involving major resource commitments or impacting long-term direction, must be even more mindful.

We need to cultivate this mindfulness and congruence, through a few strategies.

First, before actually making or committing to that big decision, stop and focus on the rationale for the decision. Management teams should answer these questions before making any big decision:

- Why are we making this choice?
- Why now?
- What do we hope to achieve?
- What are the intended goals?
- Are we thinking more about results today, or for some point in the future?
- What could be the intended, and unintended, consequences of this decision?
- What are the opportunity costs (or alternative uses of this money)?
- What is most likely to happen?
- What is the best or worst that could happen?
- Are we prepared for that outcome if things go awry?

Avoid potential decision biases, such as the present bias which focuses us on today only, at the expense of the future long-term effect. Contemplate these questions before choosing. Your employees and staff deserve that.

Then finally, make that choice and commit to it. Flawless execution is the ability to implement such decisions without errors or missteps. Follow-through is essential. Decision outcomes are not just the result of the process of choosing but also the process of implementing. Leaders must do both well.

Creating an Optimistic and Story-Based Culture

First off, great visionary leaders are also storytellers (Frei and Morriss, 2023; Bennis, 1996). **Storytelling** is the "...remarkable ability to connect people and inspire them to take action" (Frei and Morris, 2023). Storytellers are people who express their personal triumphs and failures and their vision for the future of the organization. They use narratives of the past and the future to invite people and organizations into their stories and make it about all of us, collectively. That is what makes people want to follow great leaders! Sharing stories is about two things: communicating your personal journey and sharing your vision and direction for the organization. It allows difficult marketing messages to be made clearer and for people to visualize where things are headed.

Not only does organizational purpose matter, as a strong purpose can bring people together, but storytelling further builds on this by creating stronger culture, myths, beliefs, symbols, and ideology behind the organization.

Unfortunately, most healthcare executives are not great storytellers, and they are not visionaries. Healthcare executives often get caught up in either continuing the existing culture that has been in place for many years and don't recognize they can create something novel and interesting.

Organizational culture is formally defined as the collective beliefs, values, assumptions, structure, systems, stories, and even biases that are shared by all members of the company or organization. Culture creates meaning and purpose within the organization. The culture is hard to technically measure but easy to grasp—it's the "feeling" that you get when you are working in and around that organization. Culture can be highly positive, open, transparent, innovative, growth-oriented, valuing input, and collaborative. Alternatively, it could be risk-averse, closed, cautious, stagnant, suspicious of outsiders, and so many more dimensions. That's why culture is hard to measure but one can get a good sense of the culture rather quickly. We've heard stories of new employees that say, "they didn't want to hear anything I had to say", or "they told me to not ask questions, put my head down and shut up". There are also countless stories of organizational culture where openness, friendliness, question-asking, and problem-solving are the dominant themes.

Successful leaders and entrepreneurs tend to be fairly optimistic. **Optimism** can be defined as a belief that future outcomes will usually be positive (Cambridge, 2022). Optimism is the general predisposition to be confident and upbeat, expecting good things to happen. Since all of us have general tendencies, we might either see the world as positive or dark and gloomy. Especially given these times—amidst persistent Covid, the wars in Israel or Ukraine, spiraling inflation, and a declining stock market—it is difficult to stay hopeful and positive. There is nothing right or wrong about moods or attitudes but rather they are largely just inherent human differences. But, for leaders, these dispositions are vitally important, as they could make or break your company results.

Optimism can help improve corporate culture. An optimistic environment helps to shape the stories that are being told for positive outcomes to result from the strategy and the plans. Optimism is based on your genes, or biological and genetic characteristics, but they can be influenced. We can modify our outlook and perspective with mindful diligence over time (Langabeer, 2022).

Conversely, pessimism is more about doubt, and doubt in the leader's mind can trigger doubt in employees and customers. Pessimists believe that things may not go in their favor.

Optimism is one of those traits which might put you in a better position to succeed. A recent Harvard Business Review article showed that actively encouraging positivity among your team is linked with the capacity to survive turbulence and attain better results in the long run (Achor and Gielan, 2020). This is one of numerous studies which show that a healthy dose of optimism can improve your decision quality and overall performance.

Optimism can be both taught and learned (Seligman, 2006). You can cultivate the aspects of your decisions and thoughts that are positive, or you can hire people around you that embrace the traits. To me, the basics of building an optimistic company is to first truly believe that your firm will succeed. If you don't, then you shouldn't be there. And, if you do, you should be actively spreading that news to everyone you meet—your employees, customers, and vendors. Optimism produces optimism.

Optimistic leaders tend to be good motivators. Motivating your team should be much more than just words and rewards. Building the climate that cares, that empathizes, encourages others, and allows creativity and some personal freedom is necessary today. Keeping your employees motivated will keep the climate more optimistic.

Leaders can also encourage collaborations between different units with your organization. Optimists are usually people-centric, and this boosts a spirit of collaboration. Collaboration tends to yield better results than silos and solos.

But the question remains, how do you develop this mindset if you don't already have it? Well, one great way is to utilize an executive or leadership coach to help you. Coaches work on "you" as much as the company. The key is to learn and embrace a more optimistic mindset, without becoming unrealistic or minimizing serious personal issues. Staying in integrity with your leadership style, meeting your employees where they are, and encouraging a strong belief in your company's values will create success. Excessive or false optimism, however, can create an exuberance bias in how you make decisions. If you are excessively optimistic in your beliefs, you might take risks that are not prudent or sound and can create a culture of toxic positivity, where your employees feel undervalued.

Entrepreneurial Thinking

An **entrepreneur** is typically defined as somebody that starts a new business or company. Entrepreneurs usually have a little higher tolerance for risk than most people, because rather than working for an established organization in return for a paycheck, their entire income is at risk and based on their own productivity and innovation. There are hundreds of new entrants into the healthcare space each year, typically revolving around information systems, biotechnology, medical devices, and smaller patient care facilities.

Large non-profit healthcare organizations sometimes spin off entrepreneurial units to test if those ideas and products can scale and generate higher returns. There are dozens of examples of hospitals creating prototype products and launching small businesses around them. Massachusetts General Hospital, for example, spun off a gene-editing firm that hopes to work with pharmaceutical companies to develop new gene-based therapies (Bruce, 2022). The New York-based Hospital for Special Surgery recently launched a for-profit virtual physical therapy company called RightMove Health, through a $21 million round of venture capital financing (Burky, 2022). There are dozens or hundreds of these types of launches each year.

Entrepreneurs usually have high degrees of energy, motivation, risk tolerance, and confidence. Successful entrepreneurs also have good judgment, value speed in decision-making, and are naturally curious (HBR, 2018). Entrepreneurs also appreciate change and know how to disrupt the status quo. Innovation and change are essential to being entrepreneurial, and healthcare organizations need a healthy dose of it to overcome bureaucracy and excessively structured processes that are the antithesis of growth and innovation.

These are exactly the types of skills that healthcare leaders should adapt. Even if you are not destined to launch a new business, entrepreneurial skills are highly valuable within organizations. You might be tapped to create a new service line, develop a standalone department that didn't exist before, be put in charge of a first-of-its-kind committee, or launch a novel product. In all these cases, having entrepreneurial characteristics can be highly valuable.

If you are developing and innovating internally, you might be called an **intrapreneur**.

Intrapreneurs Unlock Innovation Internally

Most of the research on entrepreneurs show propensity for higher capacity for risk-taking (Hvide and Panos, 2014). Higher risk tolerance is related to a higher likelihood of entrepreneurialism. So, risk, optimism, and new venture-seeking are all related for you as the founder or leader. But, what about your organization? Most people these days are seeing lots of job opportunities, rising wages, and flexible work structures, so they are much more likely today to consider outside options and find a new position. How do we create optimism for our own business outlook within the organization?

In today's highly competitive healthcare landscape, we as leaders of healthcare organizations must constantly innovate to stay relevant and profitable. That sounds easy but look around most large companies and you will find bureaucracy, redundant structure and policies, and waste and errors at all levels. While many organizations focus on optimizing their existing products and processes, long-term growth lies in harnessing innovation. One powerful approach to driving innovation is through intrapreneurship, which involves nurturing entrepreneurial thinking within the organization. The essence of strategic thinking lies in the ability to harness internal innovation and intrapreneurship and integrate it into their overall systems and processes.

Intrapreneurship can be defined as a people-centric, bottom-up approach to developing radical innovations within an established organization. Unlike traditional entrepreneurship, which involves starting a new external venture from scratch, intrapreneurs operate within existing organizational structures and leverage the company's resources. They are driven by a desire to create value through new products, processes, and ways of running the business. Intrapreneurship is not limited to startups, but it can thrive within large corporations as well.

Benefits of Being Entrepreneurial

Embracing intrapreneurship can yield numerous benefits for organizations. First and foremost, it fosters a culture of innovation and creativity, which leads to the development of breakthrough products and services. Intrapreneurs bring fresh perspectives and ideas to the table, challenging the status quo and pushing the boundaries of what is possible. This not only drives growth but also enhances the company's competitive advantage.

Additionally, leaders who cultivate an environment of intrapreneurship will be able to attract and retain top talent. Intrapreneurs are motivated by autonomy, the opportunity to make a significant impact, and the freedom to pursue their unique ideas. By providing an environment that supports intrapreneurial thinking, companies can create a breeding ground for talented individuals who thrive on innovation. This, in turn, strengthens the organization's ability to adapt to market changes and stay ahead of the competition.

The Leadership Challenge

Building an intrapreneurial culture starts with identifying and recognizing the entrepreneurial potential within the organization. Intrapreneurs already exist within the company; they just need to be discovered and encouraged. Research shows that more than 20% of employees exhibit entrepreneurial activity to some extent. Ignoring their efforts or stifling their ideas due to fear of disrupting the established order can hinder innovation and hinder the attraction of entrepreneurial talent.

To identify intrapreneurs, executives need to keep their eyes and ears open. Intrapreneurs are often individuals who exhibit high levels of self-confidence, autonomy, critical thinking, and decision-making ability. They are proactive, networked, and problem solvers. They are willing to take risks and challenge the status quo. By evaluating these traits systematically, leaders and human resource departments can identify potential intrapreneurs and support their development.

Creating an entrepreneurial environment requires a different management approach. Traditional hierarchical structures and rigid processes will most definitely stifle the entrepreneurial spirit and cause good people to find employment elsewhere. Executives must provide the necessary support, resources, and autonomy for intrapreneurs to thrive. This involves giving employees the freedom to experiment, supporting their initiatives, and providing guidance and mentorship along the way.

Successful intrapreneurship also requires a shift in mindset from solely focusing on efficiency and optimization to embracing calculated risk-taking and a tolerance for failure. Managers must create a safe space for intrapreneurs to test and iterate on their ideas, recognizing that failure is an essential part of the innovation process. By championing intrapreneurial efforts and celebrating both successes and failures, managers can foster a culture of continuous learning and growth.

Overcoming Challenges and Building a Culture of Innovation

While innovation and entrepreneurialism offer significant benefits, it is not without its challenges. Established organizations often face resistance to change and a preference for familiar and mature solutions. To overcome these challenges, companies must actively work to break free from the familiarity, maturity, and propinquity traps that hinder disruptive innovation.

Intrapreneurship requires a different mindset and a willingness to take calculated risks. It involves empowering employees to challenge the status quo, experiment with new ideas, and learn from failures. Companies can incentivize intrapreneurship by establishing programs that provide funding, resources, and recognition for intrapreneurial initiatives. By creating a supportive environment that encourages risk-taking and rewards innovation, organizations can unlock the full potential of their intrapreneurs.

Chapter Summary

- Leaders help make strategic decisions, but they also create positive and optimistic culture that values both innovation and creativity.
- Leaders recruit internal entrepreneurs to help them overcome complex processes and re-shape plans and strategies.

- Executives should foster the entrepreneurial mindset of employees to help develop breakthrough products, foster a culture of creativity, attract top talent, and gain a competitive edge in the market.
- It doesn't matter if your organization is non-profit or profit-maximizing—innovation, storytelling, optimism, and cultural competency are all good for performance management and competitive advantage.

Discussion Questions

1. How would you best describe your organization's culture, and how can you as a leader or manager influence that culture?
2. Does your organization value entrepreneurialism? Is innovation both allowed and encouraged? If not, does that work for the organization or what can be changed?
3. How can you, as an emerging leader or an established one, develop competencies around innovation, intrapreneurialism, and storytelling?

Key Terms

Behavioral Congruence; Behavioral Economics; Entrepreneur; Habits; Heuristics; Hunches; Innovation; Intrapreneur; Organizational Culture; Storytelling

References

Achor S and Gielan M (2020). What leading with optimism really looks like. *Harvard Business Review*, June 4, 2020. Available at https://hbr.org/2020/06/what-leading-with-optimism-really-looks-like

Bennis W (1996). The leader as storyteller. *Harvard Business Review*, 74, 1–6.

Bruce G (2022). Gene-editing Spinoff led by Mass General Brigham Veterans. *Becker's Hospital Review*, November 17, 2022. Available at https://www.beckershospitalreview.com/innovation/gene-editing-spinoff-led-by-mass-general-brigham-veterans.html

Burky A (2022). Hospital for special surgery scores $21M to spin off virtual physical therapy platform. Fierce Healthcare. Available at https://www.fiercehealthcare.com/telehealth/hospital-special-surgery-scored-21m-series-funding-spin-virtual-physical-therapy

Cambridge Dictionary. Definition of optimism. Retrieved June 8, 2022. Available at https://dictionary.cambridge.org/us/dictionary/english/optimism

Frei F and Morriss A (2023). Storytelling that drives bold change. *Harvard Business Review*, 101, 1–17.

HBR (2018). *Harvard Business Review Entrepreneur's Handbook: Everything You Need to Launch and Grow Your New Business*. Boston, FL: HBR Press.

Hvide HK and Panos GA (2014). Risk tolerance and entrepreneurship. *Journal of Financial Economics, 111*(1), 200–223.

Langabeer J (2022). Cultivating optimism and leadership in your small business. *Forbes*, July 14, 2022. Available at https://www.forbes.com

Seligman MEP (2006). *Learned Optimism: How to Change Your Mind and Your Life*. New York: Vintage Books.

Chapter 8

Governance and Boards

Governance Basics

All publicly owned companies, and most non-profits and small businesses, have a board of directors that participate in the most strategic decisions facing the firm. Even as the chief executive officer (CEO), you can't buy a new business, build an office building, or significantly alter your capital investments without additional oversight coming from a board of directors. The activities, decision processes, and systems used to effectively provide oversight and financial accountability for the organization is termed **governance**, derived from the word govern or manage. Board of directors are usually seen as the legal custodians for an organization.

Members of these boards are typically called **directors** in for-profit firms or governors or trustees in the non-profit sector. They direct resources and directly control the most strategic decisions of the organization, thus their name. The lead director is called the **board chair**, and they are responsible for the agenda and facilitating the meeting, voting, and decision processes. Typically, major decisions require either consensus or a majority to be approved. Meeting **minutes** are the official written record of that meeting, which need to be maintained for both legal and control purposes.

Non-profit healthcare organizations typically have larger boards, less involvement in setting strategy and implementation, and are primarily concerned about the social impact that the organization is having on a community. Non-profit boards have a large fundraising and business development priority, helping to raise funds for the organization.

DOI: 10.4324/9781032623726-10

On for-profit company boards, they are usually smaller and more focused on internal controls and financial performance. **Fiduciary** responsibilities involve trust and doing what is in the best financial interest of the organization, not themselves personally. Even privately held firms often have a small group of advisers they trust to serve as fiduciaries. The board of directors oversee executive management of a company and play a central role in oversight, audits, and strategic decision-making. Look at Twitter's (now "X") board role in the acquisition they faced by Elon Musk. The board of directors was very instrumental in communicating with shareholders, designing share pricing strategies, and approving or rejecting Musk's offer. In response, when Musk finally acquired the company, he terminated all nine directors (Seal, 2022).

Although most boards are either elected by a majority of shareholders (in the case of public companies) or appointed by the company leaders themselves (private companies), boards often are overlooked and under-utilized. The most important decision that boards can make is the hiring and firing of the CEO. They retain the power to replace the CEO when they are not meeting the goals and objectives, have violated financial practices, performed unethically, or for any other reason.

Governance Roles

Traditionally, CEO is the primary point of communication and alignment with the boards. In healthcare, the CEO might hold a position on the board. If not, they would be the primary executive that provides regular updates on strategic performance, typically on a monthly or quarterly basis. Boards are usually presented with financial reports, updates on strategic objectives and capital investments, major changes in the organization's operations, and whether internal accounting and management controls are working.

Since most boards bring together a wealth of expertise, they have enormous potential to provide creative, strategic input on the objectives and goals. Yet, most exercise only fiduciary control responsibility. Despite the talent and time committed, directors are not always engaged or informed enough to actively contribute. CEOs should harness the board for strategic counsel and input. It is easy to get the board mired in details such as sales funnels and product pipelines. If aligned properly, the board can play a much more significant role.

The CEO is pivotal in determining if the board is effective, or weak, as they typically control what gets presented at board meetings. A CEO or executive who works with boards needs to have a leadership style that meshes with the board and provides the information requested quickly. In this section, we will discuss how to improve board governance.

Building Better Boards

Significant research exists on how to improve the structural components of a board of directors (Charan, 2005). **Board structure**—such as board composition, rules, and procedures—is important. They help us determine which demographic and cultural background, gender, professional experience, and number of directors would be a good fit for the board for example. But this isn't enough. There are many other areas that are often neglected. Truly effective boards are used as a strategic advantage. Given their background and experience, directors often are much more seasoned at leading a business than the CEO. The key is how to tap into this effectively.

Many CEOs and executive teams have a sort of quasi-trust relationship with the board. Share too much information, and some feel it can be used against you. But don't share enough, and you are seen as withholding critical information. Some CEOs are highly deferential and subservient, while in other cases, the CEO feels they are ultimately in charge of the board. The board will determine what they will allow and what they aren't willing to accept.

Many organizational leadership teams over-hype their results, revenue potential, and treat the board as more of a "customer" or investor. This is especially true of non-profit boards. Rather than seeing the board as a true strategic partner, information is often guarded, or held closely, which limits the board's effectiveness.

Increasingly, how an organization manages the risks and opportunities related to environmental issues, social issues, and governance (sometimes called ESG), is also becoming more relevant and important in board rooms.

Six Factors that Create Better Board Governance

A good board–CEO relationship is cultivated over time and with continuous communication. Trust is highly important. The keys to making your board effective boil down to six "C's" (Langabeer, 2023) and are shown in Figure 8.1.

The first of these is **composition**, which refers to the structure and functioning of the board. This is probably the most talked about aspect of boards. Think through how diverse your board is, from a skills, gender, racial, and

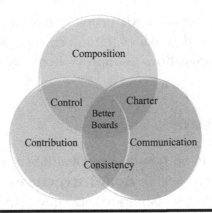

Figure 8.1 Better board governance roles.

experience perspective. Consider the size as well. Smaller boards generally are more engaged, while larger boards might be better if you have multiple committees. Larger boards are usually more diverse but often less effective.

The second is **charter**, which refers to the mission or purpose that the board officially holds beyond the fiduciary basics and hiring and firing the CEO. The charter, or purpose, could even involve directors getting directly involved in operations. It's not likely, but the charge needs to be laid out. While the board chair determines the agenda, the working relationship with the chief executive helps to outline what the executive team feels are priorities in terms of strategies, performance, or direction. The relationship between the Chair and the CEO is vital in this regard. Set a charter focused on strategic performance and direction, as well as control.

Next is the **communication** processes involved in transferring information both directions between the board and the management team. What is the level of information symmetry between the executive team and the board? Is the board getting all the necessary strategic information necessary to properly govern? Do they feel they could use more in any given area? Proactively providing directors with all the information needed in advance will help ensure better use of their time at meetings. Routinely ask the board if what they are given is trusted, valuable, and sufficient. And, the opposite is also true. The board needs to ensure that they are informing and communicating transparently to the CEO about their concerns and priorities.

Consistency, or uniformity, of the information and governance process builds better results. Boards that meet more routinely and are provided in advance the right level of information are much more likely to help provide strategic input and value than those which lack consistency. Having more frequent meetings requires more time but also builds stronger bonds while infrequent meetings are typically consumed with routine catch-ups on less strategic matters.

Contribution is the effectiveness that boards bring by actively contributing, being engaged, and adding value. Directors want to feel their time is contributing to the company. Most directors of company boards will tell you they could contribute much more than they currently are. Executives need to help boards become better engaged and forward-looking. Boards must feel comfortable knowing that they have the right and capability to address big problems or opportunities by bringing these forward to the board chair and the executive team.

Lastly, the **control** processes involve the board's primary role. Boards hold the ultimate fiduciary responsibility. Their power lies in the capacity to control key decisions around CEO hiring and firing, oversight of financials, and other controls. Make sure your board has processes and infrastructure to properly control the business.

Empowerment and Leadership

The concept of empowerment also comes into play with boards. Boards can empower their CEO by providing specific autonomy and decision rights. **Decision rights** identify the types of decisions that can be made to align with strategy, who can make those decisions, what spending limit they are authorized for, and who will be involved in making them.

Case 8.1: Sarasota Metro Devices

Sarasota Metro Devices (SMD) is a major player in the medical device industry, serving as a manufacturer of multiple specialty medical devices. SMD has a board of directors, comprised of four people: two had an initial investment in the firm when it was founded in 2005, and the other two are friend of theirs. The CEO does not have a role on the board but is very active in providing all of the information and reporting out at board meetings.

The Chief Strategy Officer (CSO) was concerned that the company was getting a little stale in their approach to new products and was not keeping up with competition. The CEO agreed and had brought this to the attention of the board multiple times, requesting significant capital investment to build out facilities for new product lines. The CSO had also identified an opportunity for the acquisition of another small competitor that might provide immediate market share in these new, more profitable product lines.

At the last quarterly board meeting, this was discussed again, and the directors decided not to pursue either of these options, with the belief that they did not have the capital and did not want to further leverage the company with debt. A few years later, SMD declared bankruptcy and was acquired by a national firm for about 50% of its market value from just 2 years earlier.

What went wrong with their board and strategic direction? Lack of broad, diverse representation is one factor. Not having the CEO as a voting board member was another issue. Board members have a critical fiduciary responsibility to not just maintain status quo but to be forward-looking for opportunities to grow and maintain their competition position. In this case, SMD's board was partially to blame for the company's eventual downfall.

Board Effectiveness Reviews

If you're the CEO or board chair, one simple way to gauge whether you are doing a good job engaging the board is to ask each director this simple question: "do you feel you are contributing 100% of your talents in this role?" And, if the answer is "no", be prepared to step up and make some changes in your board's overall roles. Similarly, routinely asking directors "what else can we do to give you the information you need to best do your role?" would provide useful insight. Board effectiveness questionnaires (or audits) should gauge not only their perceived level of oversight but access to critical information and the level of trust with the team.

In order to build strong governance processes, you should consider an annual full **board effectiveness assessment**, sometimes called an audit, which would help evaluate the board's contributions and overall effectiveness. This assessment would involve a questionnaire, or individual interviews with each director, to assess their perceptions of how the board is functioning with regards to communication, consistency, control, charter, composition, and contributions. The board should feel open and candid enough to provide direct feedback to the CEO and the Chair about how to improve in these areas and to improve the oversight it provides. Board reviews are best done by independent parties, not the CEO or another management team member. An external management consultant can help provide these reviews. Allow the review to guide changes in governance, as well as organizational management.

Cultivating a more engaged and effective board of directors will positively influence your future company results. CEOs and other healthcare leaders must learn how to work with board members, build a spirit of trust and collaboration, and leverage director's experience and background to provide better strategic direction for the organization.

Chapter Summary

- Board of directors are instrumental in both fiduciary and strategic control of an organization.
- Trust, collaboration, and empowerment are key to a successful working relationship between the CEO and the board.
- While the primary purpose of the board is to maintain controls, hire and fire the CEO, and set strategic priorities, they can be useful in other ways.
- Environmental, social, and governance (ESG) issues are increasingly important for executives and board members.
- There are six C's that can help improve board governance: composition, charter, communication, consistency, contribution, and control.
- Board effectiveness assessments should be conducted at least annually to review the board's overall level of functioning.

Discussion Questions

1. Who is on your organization's board of directors? What expertise do they bring?
2. What level of strategic input does the board have on your planning and execution processes?
3. Do board directors feel they are contributing and adding value within your organization?

Key Terms

Board Chair; Board Effectiveness Assessment; Board of Directors; Board Structure; Charter; Composition; Communication; Consistency; Control; Contribution; Decision Rights; Directors; Fiduciary; Governance; Minutes

References

Charan R (2005). *Boards that Deliver. Advancing Corporate Governance from Compliance to Competitive Advantage.* New York: Jossey-Bass Publishers.
Langabeer J (2023). The 6 C's of cultivating more effec-
    tive boards. Forbes.com, August 15, 2022. Available at https://
    www.forbes.com/sites/forbesbusinesscouncil/2022/08/15/
    the-6-cs-for-cultivating-a-more-engaged-and-effective-board-of-directors
Seal D (2022). Elon Musk Ousts Twitter Board, Named Sole Director. Wall Street
    Journal, October 31, 2022. Available at https://www.wsj.com/articles/
    musk-ousts-twitter-board-named-sole-director-11667234297.

Chapter 9

Growth Strategies

Three Forms of Growth

For many healthcare entities, the overarching strategy tends to focus on growth—growing revenues, customer base, employees, and profitability. Board of directors often mandate growth to ensure the entity is further developing over time and capturing higher levels of market share. Growth is usually perceived as an indicator of how well the organization is doing in the market and is often a key metric for how c-level employees are incentivized.

There are three main types of growth strategies that firms can pursue. The first is **organic growth**. Organic growth occurs when you get a new customer for existing facilities, relying on your own existing resources. The second involves **strategic alliances** or partnerships with external entities. And the third is through **mergers** or **acquisitions**.

Organic growth is largely the standard process by which an organization grows their own operations internally using internal capabilities and resources. However, there are limits to which organizations can organically grow. Most can't scale their information systems and human resources sufficiently to grow beyond a small percentage each year. One study showed that the most an organization can expect to grow would be around 1% greater than the gross domestic product, or in other words, 3%–7% growth year over year (Mackey and Valikangas, 2004). There are just practical limits on unbounded growth. It would be nearly impossible for example to double in size in a span of just a few years. Firms would not be able to recruit the

DOI: 10.4324/9781032623726-11

right talent, build the right facilities, or scale the systems and processes to handle that much growth organically.

However, there are many advantages of organic growth, such as:

■ It provides deeper first-hand knowledge that is likely to be internalized in the company.
■ It helps spread investment over time and reduce upfront commitment.
■ There are no availability constraints, which means they are not dependent on the availability of suitable acquisition targets or potential alliance partners to grow.
■ The organization remains independent and in control of its own future.
■ The creation of new activities within the existing culture environment can often spur growth in big ways.

The downside is that organic growth can be very slow, and for organizations that need to radically transform or change their margins or other metrics, this might not be an option. It's also limited to existing internal capabilities and resources.

Strategic alliances are contractual arrangements between multiple organizations to undertake a mutually beneficial set of projects, or even a new business entity, with each organization retaining its independence. Strategic alliances are very common in healthcare, with partnerships between medical schools and hospitals for example or pharmaceutical and biotech companies. Strategic alliances require extensive coordination and strong leadership. Branding, market entry, and investment returns are the major factors in the use of alliances.

Strategic alliances are partnerships, for example when multiple companies both allocate resources to work toward a common goal or strategy. In essence, two or more independent organizations would pursue a joint objective, such as opening a new service line independent of each firm. Or, maybe a new product creation. Any new product or service might be co-owned (called an equity alliance or a joint venture), or they might be just committed on paper or contractually to work together based on assignment of cost and profit percentages. The advantages of alliances are that they are typically easier to form, less costly than direct investments, and require less commitment and possibly risks. The downsides are that the lack of unified control tends to make them less manageable and sustainable, and many fail. People often falsely believe that strategic alliances are easier to manage than a merger or acquisition, but in fact they are much more unwieldy. Alliances,

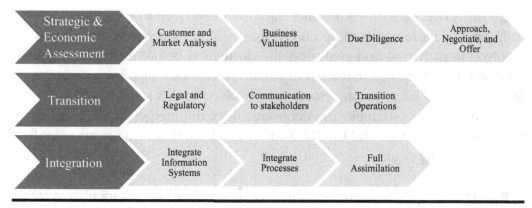

Figure 9.1 M&A growth process.

such as joint ventures, have their purposes, for entering new markets or launching a product, but they may not be the best strategy for all organizational growth.

The third type of growth strategy is through a merger or an acquisition. A merger is the combining of two organizations entirely, while an acquisition is an outright purchase of one firm by another. Both involve combining systems, processes, customers, and employees into one common organization. This is technically difficult, given the scale of most organizations today. It is not easy to move all vendors or procurement orders into one system or combine two different payroll systems. Even more difficult is getting all patients onto one common electronic health record.

Mergers and acquisitions (M&A) involves three basic phases. The strategic and economic analysis is stage 1. Transitioning the processes, procedures, systems, employees, vendors, and customers or patients is stage 2. And, then full integration, or assimilation into the enterprise, is stage 3. Figure 9.1 shows these graphically.

Strategic and Economic Analyses

If the organization has chosen to go down the M&A path, there are some strategic considerations before they acquire or be merged. Executives must think through the "fit" or alignment between the two companies. They must also ensure the financials are correct, and there is a good estimate of the economic value of both organizations. Maybe the M&A might bring increased number of customers. A detailed review should be conducted to make sure the numbers provided in the deal are "real". Surprisingly, a number of small firms overstate their customer base, so these need to be audited carefully. Finally, there needs to be due diligence. Due diligence is the process involved in gathering and analyzing all information before making a decision on that transaction, to avoid legal or financial liabilities. Multiple executives from finance to information systems get involved in this stage of M&A.

To really assess strategic and economic fit of the merger or acquisition, the board of directors and the CEO should address these questions prior to engaging in any deal:

- Does this combination of organizations improve our competitiveness? What about our market share, our price, our profitability?
- Do we gain novel or unique products or services, or new locations served?
- Are we able to enter a new market?
- Do we fend off existing competitors with this combination?
- What is all this worth financially? What level of debt are we willing to incur to make this happen?
- How will this combination fit with, and impact, our organizational culture?
- Can we pull off a transition plan and integration flawlessly?
- Do we have the right resources (human, financial, information, facilities) to make this integration seamless to our customers and patients?
- Are all of the numbers (customer/patient count, accounts receivable estimate, annual expenses, staffing numbers, etc.) correct and verifiable?
- Does pursuing this deal make us not pursue another viable path?
- Is this justifiable legally (to the US Department of Justice)? Will it create regulatory challenges for us?
- Which strategic alternative is best for us, financially and for all other measures of organizational health?
- What is the appropriate economic valuation we are willing to invest to make this deal happen?

Once the potential deal has been thoroughly evaluated, an offer is typically made, followed by extensive negotiations, and then a final price is confirmed. There are a lot of details that need to be worked out by all functions within both organizations, and this list is not complete. Only if the management team can satisfactorily address these questions (and more), and remain optimistic about the combination of the two organizations, should a merger or an acquisition proceed to the next stage.

Transition Plans

Stage 2 of the M&A process is to prepare and begin working on a complete transition plan. A **transition plan** is the set of steps and activities necessary to prepare for the full integration. Transitioning means to transfer all or some part of the acquired organization's processes, procedures, systems, employees, vendors, and customers or patients into the new organization. Imagine something simple, such as appointment scheduling. Which website link should we use for the combined organization? What set of phone numbers will survive, and which ones need to be transferred so that it is seamless to the customers/patients of the other organization. Transition plans are all about making the full integration occur without incident, errors, or losses to the customers, vendors, and patients.

Post-merger training and communication for all key staff and managers is necessary to address the questions that inevitably will come up. Strategic leaders are as transparent as they can be during these times, which usually involve both legal and financial confidentiality on both parts. But once deals are intended to move forward, communication and transparency are required. All employees need to be aware of their role in the transition and the post-M&A new enterprise.

During this stage, it is essential that leaders rely on outside experts—consultants who have gone through a similar process to share what they know and a thorough roadmap for transitioning. Transition plans will help guide the process and address all areas of marketing, legal, financial, systems, physician relations, media relations, and other functions prior to any full integration.

Integration

The final stage is full integration, involving combining of both firms into one new entity. Integration is when transition plans are put in place. Changes are made based on the plans, and it is essential that leaders utilize change management techniques to make newly acquired employees feel comfortable, existing customers welcomed, and all others well-informed.

M&A involves shifts in the business model and collective processes. Therefore, managing the effect of this change on employees can help improve retention and overall buy-in. Altering the mindset of individuals impacted is time-consuming but necessary to reach full potential of any big restructuring or consolidation (Andersen, 2022). **Change management** are the activities involved in helping people adapt to change. Change management techniques will focus on improving communication to increase understanding the impact of change, clarifying goals and expectations, listening to employee's suggestions and recommendations, measuring the extent of change, engaging and training employees on new processes and systems, reinforcing priorities, and building trust and a positive culture.

While the potential benefits of M&A in the healthcare industry are substantial, organizations must navigate the complexities of the M&A journey effectively. Successful execution of M&A requires careful planning, robust due diligence, and meticulous integration efforts. It is crucial to establish a clear strategic rationale, align cultures and values, and create a well-defined integration roadmap to maximize the value derived from the transaction.

Full assimilation or integration is stage 3, but this stage can go on for many months. That is why Chapter 10 focuses on flawless execution. Transitions lead to integration, and integrations lead to operational day-to-day implementation.

Growth Strategy

M&A can help unlock synergies, optimize resources, and capitalize on new opportunities. They can help grow the **service lines**, or discrete group of closely related services offered, for an organization. Yet, they are complicated and difficult to finance and move through all stages. Some years, there is a huge volume of deals in the healthcare industry. However, due to the Corona Virus of 2019 (COVID-19), the number and size of M&A transactions was significantly down in years 2021 through 2023. Modern Healthcare (2023) maintains a database of all M&A transactions over time. The trend has slowly decreased during COVID years, but recent research suggests that a resurgence in activity is expected (McKinsey, 2024; Henry and Oostende 2023).

Despite the challenges posed by the pandemic, deal-making in the sector appears to be renewed, with a focus on creating strategic value, suggesting M&A could be a strategic tool for healthcare organizations. The most impacted management and staff impacted initially during stage 1 (economic analysis) are probably the CEO, Chief Financial Officer (CFO), and Chief Strategy Officer (CSO). It is possible that individuals who work with these executives will get a chance to work on an M&A, so all healthcare leaders should understand the basic process and structure of this growth strategy.

Rationale Behind Mergers and Acquisitions

Despite the complexities and costs involved in M&A, it is still a useful strategy to pursue. To understand the motivations behind M&A activity in the healthcare industry, it is essential to examine the strategic imperatives that drive such decisions, these would include:

- *Market Consolidation*: Sometimes, healthcare firms and hospitals seek to gain competitive advantage by increasing their market share. This also helps to increase service offerings and entering new geographic markets. Consolidating organizations tend to achieve economies of scale by utilizing one primary electronic health record (EHR); enterprise resource planning (ERP); and centralized processes, staff, and management systems.
- *Rapid Growth*: Sometimes, organizations need rapid growth to avoid financial distress or bankruptcy and to enter new markets and gain patient revenues or volumes. These deals represent one mechanism to rapidly grow.
- *Optimization of Service Portfolio*: Healthcare organizations often pursue M&A to optimize their portfolio of services and products. By divesting non-core assets or acquiring complementary businesses, entities can streamline their operations, focus on areas of strategic priority, and create a more cohesive value proposition. This strategic realignment enables organizations to better meet evolving customer demands and capitalize on emerging market trends.
- *Acquisition of Talent and Resources*: In an industry driven by specialized expertise, M&A can serve to attract and retain top talent. By acquiring organizations with a strong physician base or leadership with unique capabilities, healthcare entities can gain a competitive edge, foster innovation, and nurture a culture of continuous learning.

International Growth

Healthcare is not just a domestic activity. Some organizations choose to pursue M&A or organic growth internationally as well. As the healthcare industry becomes increasingly interconnected and globalized, prominent US hospitals for example are expanding their reach beyond domestic borders. This expansion is driven by a variety of factors, including the desire to tap into new markets, share expertise and knowledge in regions that lack sufficient resources, and meet the growing demand for high-quality health-care services.

Examples of international growth can be seen by many of the leading hospitals. Johns Hopkins Medicine began their international strategy with the formation of Johns Hopkins Aramco Healthcare, which is a Saudi Arabian state-owned oil company. Their strategic goal was to provide exceptional healthcare to more than 70,000 employees across Aramco (Johns Hopkins Medicine, 2023).

Cleveland Clinic, a prominent healthcare system, established its presence in London, United Kingdom, to provide specialized healthcare services (Schwartz, 2023). The University of Texas MD Anderson Cancer Center has opened centers and created partnerships for operations in Singapore and Africa, as well as other regions (MD Anderson, 2023). The Mayo Clinic, a top-ranked academic medical center in Minnesota, has claims to have more than 40 global partners across the world, including London (Mayo Clinic, 2023). They also provide global consulting around improving healthcare services as well. Many others are also working on international expansion as a way to grow organically, or through strategic alliances.

Clearly, the international expansion of hospitals reflects a paradigm shift in healthcare delivery, driven by the pursuit of global collaboration, knowledge sharing, and the provision of high-quality care to diverse populations.

Motivations and Intent Behind International Growth

The motivations behind US hospitals expanding their operations globally are multifaceted. These hospitals seek to:

- Expand access to high-quality care: By establishing international locations, US hospitals aim to provide access to their renowned healthcare services to patients who may otherwise have limited options for specialized care in their home countries. This expansion allows patients to benefit from advanced treatments, cutting-edge technologies, and the expertise of highly skilled healthcare professionals.
- Foster new and collaborative partnerships: International ventures enable hospitals to forge collaborative partnerships with local healthcare providers, government entities, and academic institutions. Through these partnerships, knowledge transfer, research collaboration, and best practice sharing can occur, contributing to advancements in healthcare delivery and improving patient outcomes.

■ Enhance brand reputation: Establishing a global presence allows US hospitals to strengthen their brand reputation and position themselves as leaders in the field. By delivering high-quality care and achieving successful outcomes, these hospitals can attract patients and physicians from around the world, solidifying their standing as trusted healthcare providers.

■ Create new forms of revenue: International expansion presents an opportunity for US hospitals to diversify their revenue streams and mitigate risks associated with a single market. By tapping into new markets and attracting international patients, these hospitals can generate additional revenue and support their mission of delivering exceptional patient care and advancing medical research.

■ Contribute to improving global health: Healthcare organizations can contribute to global health initiatives and address healthcare challenges on a broader scale. By collaborating with local healthcare systems, these hospitals can support capacity building, improve healthcare infrastructure, and help address specific health concerns prevalent in different regions.

International expansion is just one way health organizations can grow and expand.

Chapter Summary

■ There are three primary forms of organizational growth: Organic, strategic alliances, and mergers and acquisitions.

■ M&A transactions, or deals, are able to quickly increase revenue and scale relative to the other two options.

■ Healthcare M&A has decreased significantly during COVID-19 years but is expected to increase.

■ Before engaging in any M&A transaction, senior leadership and board members must ask themselves a set of strategic and financial questions.

■ The three primary stages of M&A are economic analysis, transition, and integration.

■ Leading healthcare organizations are increasingly looking beyond their primary community and expanding internationally.

Discussion Questions

1. What type of growth rate is built into your organization's strategic plan?
2. Have you been part of a merger or an acquisition? What was your impression of how that transpired?
3. How seamless or flawless do you believe the integration and consolidation of two disparate systems can really be? What steps would you take during the transition to prepare for this?
4. Is your organization working internationally? How do the different cultures work together?

Key Terms

Acquisitions; Change Management; Mergers; Organic Growth; Strategic Alliances; Transition Plan

References

Andersen E (2022). Change is hard. Here's how to make it less painful. *Harvard Business Review*, reprint H06Y5L, April 7, 2022. Available at HBR.org

Johns Hopkins Medicine (2023). Johns Hopkins Medicine International. Information extracted from website. Accessed on November 12, 2023. Available at https://www.hopkinsmedicine.org/international

Henry J and Oostende M (2023). Signs of optimism in the M&A market. May 16, 2023. Report available at https://www.mckinsey.com/capabilities/m-and-a/our-insights/signs-of-optimism-in-the-m-and-a-market

Mackey J and Valikangas L (2004). The Myth of unbounded growth. *Sloan Management Review*, January 15, 2004.

Mayo Clinic (2023). Mayo Clinic Global Presence. Information extracted from website. Accessed on November 12, 2023. Available at https://www.mayoclinic.org

McKinsey (2024). What to expect in US healthcare in 2024 and beyond. January 5, 2024, p. 1–10. Available at https://www.mckinsey.com/industries/healthcare/our-insights/what-to-expect-in-us-healthcare-in-2024-and-beyond#/

MD Anderson Cancer Center (2023). Global Outreach. Information extracted from website. Accessed on November 12, 2023. Available at https://www.mdanderson.org/about-md-anderson/our-locations/md-anderson-cancer-network/global-outreach.html

Modern Healthcare (2023). Mergers and Acquisitions Transactions Database. Accessed on August 1, 2023. Available at modernhealthcare.com/data-insights/mergers-acquisitions

Schwartz N (2023). Cleveland Clinic continues international expansion, opens London facility. December 13, 2023. Available at https://www.beckershospitalreview.com/capital/cleveland-clinic-continues-international-expansion-opens-london-facility.html

STRATEGIC EXECUTION

Chapter 10

Flawless Execution

With strategy, you eventually need to implement the formulated plans. Implementation is the final phase of strategy development. The uses of the terms **implementation** and **execution** are interchangeable, and both these terms refer to the actions involved in putting your decisions and plans into effect. In other words, getting things done, achieving initiatives, and accomplishing objectives on-time. Flawless execution should be the primary goal. By **flawless execution**, we mean implementing plans nearly perfectly without a major glitch or error.

When implementations go awry, these are called failures. Strategy failures can be grouped into two major categories: (1) failure to create a robust plan that can generate unique, competitive advantage and achieve the organization's goals and objectives; and (2) failure to implement the plans appropriately (Chamorro-Premuzic and Lovric, 2022). You can have the best, most innovative strategy but not be able to put it into practice. You could also have a pretty poor plan, lethargic goals, but implement the plan perfectly. Neither would bring about good results. Imagine if the quality of your organization's strategy were plotted on a Y-axis, and the quality of your execution capabilities on the X-axis, as shown in Figure 10.1. Ideally, you want to position your organization in the top upper right quadrant.

If your team spent the appropriate amount of time collecting strategic market intelligence, analyzing the environment, and considering all available strategic options that provide unique differentiation from your competitors, you should end up with a pretty high-quality strategy. On the other spectrum, flawless execution is about being able to implement ambitious strategies by converting them into operational processes and systems. It may be easier to develop a great strategy than to implement it.

DOI: 10.4324/9781032623726-13

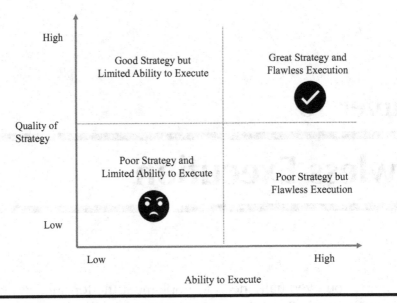

Figure 10.1 Strategy-execution matrix.

Putting Strategy into Action

How do we go about flawlessly executing our strategy, converting your well-formulated strategy and plan into actions? Here are seven things that healthcare executives should do to ensure you convert effective strategy into action.

1. Leaders define success in practical terms
2. Leaders set challenging goals and monitor progress
3. Leaders recruit and empower the right people
4. Leaders build alignment
5. Leaders reward their teams
6. Leaders remove roadblocks
7. Leaders adapt when necessary

Leaders Define Success in Practical Terms

Just like the famous Alice in Wonderland story says, "If you don't know where you're going, any road will take you there." Leaders must define what success will look like. Ask yourself: how will we know when we've achieved our strategic objectives? Make sure these are all on paper, clearly articulated, and well understood by everybody that has a role in execution.

This way you can measure and reward success appropriately. Healthcare executives should also encourage collaboration and build trust between their staff members, because ideally the entire organization is involved in flawless execution.

Leaders Set Challenging Goals and Monitor Progress

Leaders are ambitious by nature and should challenge the status quo within healthcare organizations. This is why goals that are set during the strategic plan might be highly ambitious, challenging, and are considered "stretch" goals. Your team should stretch their limits to put it in place but still get it accomplished. Leaders should take that first major step to encourage high aspirations—that's the vision and direction they would like to head. If a major retail pharmacy chain wants to double in size, the CEO doesn't need to lay out all the details to their team on the first day. But they do need to be clear about their aspirations and hopes for where the organization is headed.

Goals should also be achievable though, through some combination of direct investment in all resources (e.g., human, financial, information, time). These goals help to align the team around direction and purpose of the organization. Without a clear picture of what you're trying to attain, it can be difficult to establish a plan for getting there. One common mistake when goal setting—whether related to personal growth, professional development, or business—is setting objectives that are impossible to reach. Remember: Goals should be attainable. Setting goals that aren't realistic can lead you and your team to feel overwhelmed, uninspired, deflated, and potentially burned out. To avoid inadvertently causing low morale, review the outcomes and performances—both the successes and failures—of previous change initiatives to determine what's realistic given your timeframe and resources committed. Use this experience to define what success looks like. Another important aspect of goal setting is to account for variables that may hinder your team's ability to reach them and to lay out contingency plans. The better prepared you are, the more successful the implementation will likely be.

Once you've determined the goals you're working toward and the variables that might get in your way, you should build a roadmap for achieving those goals, set expectations among your team, and clearly communicate your implementation plan, so there's no confusion. This roadmap should include a clear delineation of roles and responsibilities. Each team member should understand what is expected of them and how their work contributes to the larger goal. By ensuring that everyone is on the same page, you can minimize confusion and reduce the risk of tasks falling through the cracks. It's also important to define relationships and communication channels within the team. Clear lines of communication can help prevent misunderstandings and ensure that everyone is working together effectively. In this phase, it can be helpful to document all of the roles, responsibilities, and relationships to create a reference point for the team. This can help new members understand their place in the team and ensure that everyone is aware of the big picture.

Once the goals and timeline are in place, leaders need to continuously monitor progress with their teams, looking to keep projects and objectives on-track. Stay updated with the implementation team to stay informed and provide direction when necessary.

Leaders Recruit and Empower the Right People

As an executive, your managers and key staff oversee implementing the strategic objectives and goals. You have to pick the right people! Recruiting and hiring the right people is one thing, but then you have to give them appropriate structure and autonomy to do what they feel is necessary to implement. This can be complex.

We recommend you assess your leadership team around you. Do you have the right human capital to get this strategy implemented flawlessly? Do you have somebody that others trust and listen to? Do you have somebody that excels at project management? Somebody good at communication and inter-departmental relations? Somebody strong with finance, marketing, or supply chain? Each of these roles is necessary to implement flawlessly. Then, map their roles to the capabilities required to get implementation done correctly. Use the balanced scorecard and strategy map routinely so each manager can see how they fit in and what they are responsible for achieving.

Empowerment involves passing authority and control on to others in your team. Have you empowered those responsible for execution to get the job done correctly? Start there, but you also might need to hire new talent or recruit from other departments. Gaps are common. Shore up any weaknesses to ensure flawless execution of the plans.

Leaders Build Alignment and Trust

Leaders and executives who execute well know that the entire organization, internal and external—including your board of directors, advisers, customers, patients, supply chain partners, and others—need to be in **alignment** (or in harmony and synchronized) with your decisions and plans. Leaders are trustworthy, and build trust within their organizations. If you decide you are about to double in size, but forgot to bring the Chief Information Officer or his staff into the conversation until the final day, you won't have a system in place that can accommodate the enterprise.

Management systems help to keep organizations in alignment, balanced, and in control. Kaplan and Norton (2006) define a management system as "a set of processes and practices used to align and control an organization. These include procedures for planning strategy and operations, for setting capital and operating budgets, for measuring and rewarding performance, and for reporting progress and conducting meetings."

Leaders need to define what management systems they currently have in place and design new ones that allow for better strategy design and flawless execution.

Leaders Reward Their Team

Successful executives should be tying managers and staff compensation and incentives to their achievement of the strategic goals and objectives. While this happens in some types of healthcare organizations (e.g., for-profit pharmaceuticals for example), it is relatively uncommon in hospitals or clinics. There, executives might be using outdated human resource processes that don't financially or otherwise incentivize their team for hitting objectives. Does your organization pay most employees only their straight salary? What about key personnel? There must be an incentive mechanism in place to keep people happy and aligned with the strategic objectives.

Leaders Remove Obstacles

We all know that there will be obstacles or roadblocks to flawless execution. These could be any number of things, such as:

- Lack of organizational buy-in or support
- Negative attitudes of certain staff members
- Outdated business processes
- Competition for time or resources
- Lack of inter-departmental collaboration
- Turnover of key personnel
- Lack of adoption of practices
- Poor quality of facilities

There are probably dozens of other roadblocks you and your teams might face, but as a healthcare executive, spend quality time working with your team, reviewing operational challenges and empowering others to help remove organizational obstacles to solidify flawless execution.

Leaders Adapt When Necessary

Finally, adaptation is sometimes necessary. A successful military officer will not just keep sending troops into a battle if they aren't seeing the results they expected. They adapt or change. It might not require adapting the plan or objectives, but the approach. Successful leaders know that they do not need to stick to a plan unnecessarily and rigidly when something is not working right.

Dig in with your operations and implementation teams to find out what is not working. Is it as simple as a lack of some important resource? Is it related to challenges with the organizational culture which is not accepting the change? Or is this something else entirely? Conduct an operational review frequently to find out from your key managers and staff how they are doing against the strategy map and timeline. Are the objectives being carried out? Are timelines being met? Great leaders conduct these types of review periodically to ensure that initiatives are successful over time.

Case 10.1: BigBox Pharmacy Inc.

BigBox Pharmacy is a national retail pharmacy that recruited a new CEO, Alison Tomas, in 2023. Alison's background included many years in the pharmaceutical manufacturing business before taking over this new role. She walked into the position, knowing that a large management consultancy had just finished working with the senior leadership team to define a new strategic plan for the next 10 years. In the plan, the compound annual growth rate for her company was projected to be 4%, whereas the vision was to nearly double that rate. The termination of the prior CEO by the board of directors was done pretty quickly after the consulting report and plan was finalized, and a search for a new CEO was initiated. Walking into this new role, she finds that the operational and store staff are fairly under-resourced. The senior managers were appropriate, but missing was a solid level of specialists under each role. In fact, nearly all of the previous strategic objectives that were being implemented were delayed by as much as 2 years. Alison determines she needs to define some concrete goals and empower the team to recruit human resource gaps immediately. She also implemented management systems that would allow her to keep a close eye on all aspects of the organization's performance toward the strategic plan. After 12 months, she feels she has a much better handle on all operations and is seeing significant improvements in the financial, customer, and internal processes.

Project Management

Flawless execution of strategic plans requires that initiatives and objectives be managed formally as a project. A **project** is an organized effort involving a sequence of activities that are temporarily being performed to achieve a desired outcome. Since they are temporary and involve a variety of individuals and activities, it is important to organize and manage projects appropriately. Similarly, the change that results from projects must be closely managed.

Project management is the application of knowledge, skills, tools, and techniques to project activities to meet the project requirements (Project Management Institute, 2023; PMBOK, 2023). The primary goal is to implement the plans <u>on-time</u> and <u>on-budget</u> and to have these become part of daily operational practices. Since all projects have a start and an end, the key to management is to successfully navigate that project through the various stages to ultimate completion and achievement of success. There are three high-level phases in project management that project managers need to understand well:

- *Project Initiation and Design.* This entails the assessment and selection of a new project and its design. This entails all aspects of project planning, which we will describe below.
- *Project Execution.* This entails the control and delivery of the project, including the management of the budget, personnel, schedules, improvement activities, and other aspects of management.
- *Project Closure.* This entails performing all the necessary organizational steps to closing out a project (such as budget, moving personnel back to assigned departments) as well as performing post-project reviews outlining the outcomes and learning opportunities which results from the project (Figure 10.2).

Keeping projects on-track, on-time, and on-budget is a primary goal. The use of project plans, such as Gantt charts, is essential (Figure 10.3).

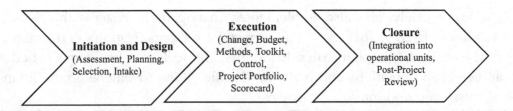

Figure 10.2 Phases in project management.

	Name	Duration	Predecessors	Resource names	December / Dec	January / Jan	February / Feb	March / Mar	April / Apr
1	⊞ Scope	3.5 d							
7	⊞ Analysis/Scope Requirements	14 d							
17	⊟ Design	14.5 d							
18	Review preliminary software specificati…	2 d	16	Analyst			Analyst		
19	Develop functional specifications	5 d	18	Analyst			Analyst		
20	Develop prototype based on functional …	4 d	19	Analyst			Analyst		
21	Review functional specifications	2 d	20	Management			Management		
22	Incorporate feedback into functional sp…	1 d	21	Management			Management		
23	Obtain approval to proceed	4 h	22	Management;Proje…			Management;Project Manager		
24	Design complete	0 d	23				2/15		
25	⊟ Development	21.75 d							
26	Review functional specifications	1 d	24	Developer			Developer		
27	Identify modular/tiered design parameters	1 d	26	Developer			Developer		
28	Assign development staff	1 d	27	Developer			Developer		
29	Develop code	15 d	28	Developer				Developer	
30	Developer testing (primary debugging)	15 d	29	Developer				Developer	
31	Development complete	0 d	30					3/16	
32	⊞ Testing	48.75 d							
48	⊞ Training	45.75 d							
57	⊞ Documentation	30.5 d							
67	⊞ Pilot	70.25 d							
74	⊞ Deployment	5 d							
81	⊞ Post Implementation Review	3 d							
86	Software development template complete	0 d	85						

Figure 10.3 Project plans (Gantt charts).

Finally, project managers should encourage the use of strategy maps to balance the objectives with operational activities, key performance indicators, and goals. This helps ensure projects stay on track. A sample strategic project framework is shown in Figure 10.4.

Managing projects is a learned skill, and leaders should appoint the right person to oversee strategic initiatives. Organizing resources and activities logically and efficiently produces more optimal results. There are numerous techniques to help design optimal sequencing of a project plan, but there are numerous threats or risks that could derail flawless execution. These should be identified and mitigated. Projects force change however, and the principles and mechanisms for managing change should be incorporated into all projects. Communication strategies with brand positioning should be included on a regular basis in all timelines, cost, service, and strategic issues related to organizational stakeholders in order to prepare and accept changes.

Strategic Project Objectives	*Become Seamless*	*Automate Processes*	*Financially Effective*	*Retain and Recruit Talent*
Operational Activities	• Attend Nursing and clinical meetings • Create service level agreements with customers • Partner with Vendors • Update Policy and Procedures manual • Forecasting Inventory	• Warehouse scanning solution • Business Intelligence Reporting	• Establish consignment inventory programs where possible	•Identify current skill sets of employees •Determine skill sets necessary for future roles •Include employee input on policies and procedures
Key Performance Indicators	• Improved communication with customers • Reduced Inventory Risk • Improved Vendor Relationships • Improved efficiencies • Reduced stock-outs	• Improved Productivity • Better Reporting to analyze costs, improve compliance, and drive standardization	• Improved inventory utilization • Reduced days inventory on hand	•Implement quarterly employee survey •Reduced loss of personnel to other departments
Goals	• Reduction in complaints >10% • Reduction in stock outs by 20%	• Decreased data entry time for requisitions >10% • Reduction in data entry errors >10%	• Inventory value for both warehouses =<$500,000 • Decreased days inventory on hand > 5 days	•Ensure each employee receives 24 hours training per year

Figure 10.4   Strategic project framework.

Chapter Summary

- The best laid plans will not succeed if they aren't executed perfectly.
- Executives should focus just as much on implementation and execution as they did with the strategic planning process.
- Flawless execution is not just about imperfection but about adapting and leading through times of change.
- Executives need to focus on creating management systems that help align and control the organization.
- Successful leaders put strategy into action by empowering, rewarding, removing roadblocks, setting challenging goals, achieving alignment, and adapting when necessary.
- Operational project management teams should be used to successfully implement plans and objectives.

Discussion Questions

1. What additional obstacles to successful implementation, beyond what was mentioned here, have you seen in practice?
2. What leadership skills do you feel you are lacking to be excellent at implementation?
3. What companies can you think of that execute flawlessly?
4. How should project risks be identified timely, and what are the most important risks you could envision?

Key Terms

Alignment; Empowerment; Flawless Execution; Implementation; Management Systems; Project; Project Management

References

Chamorro-Premuzic T and Lovric D (2022). How to move from strategy to execution. *Harvard Business Review*, Jan-February 2022. Reprint HO742V, p. 1–7.

Kaplan R and Norton D (2006). How to implement a new strategy without disrupting your organization. *Harvard Business Review, 84,* 1–10.

PMBOK (2023). *A Guide to the Project Management Body of Knowledge (PMBOK Guide)* (7th ed). Newtown Square, PA: Project Management Institute.

Project Management Institute (2023). What is Project Management? Available at www.PMI.org

Chapter 11

Managing Performance

Toward Operational Excellence

The concept of managing organizational performance after implementing a strategic plan requires that organizations understand their current and expected performance and then use processes and systems to deliver on those performance goals. In many respects, this requires that managers approach each project as a component of strategic planning process. Strategy and operations are mutually reinforcing. Most importantly, performance improvement requires knowledge about strategy, different dimensions of performance, and how to establish performance targets. Performance management is key to long-term change. All of these will be described in this chapter.

Performance Management

Organizations continuously seek to improve their performance. **Performance management** refers to the process by which organizations implement their strategies and align their resources, systems, and employees to strategic objectives. The goal is **operational excellence**, which is a uniform practice of delivering on goals, triggering the entire organization to continuously do better on a daily basis (Langabeer and Helton, 2020). And this doesn't just apply to profit-seeking firms. Non-profit and governmental healthcare organizations are not exempt from this process of managing toward strategic goals. Hospitals and health systems obviously exist for many reasons, such as to heal the sick, to improve the health of the community, and to research new treatments. The core services provided within health organizations typically include observation, diagnosis, treatment, and rehabilitation. Notice that these all revolve around patient and the public's health—which can be measured clinically or medically. Quality measures and medical outcomes could be used to assess if the health system did a reasonable job in improving customer, operational, or financial metrics.

Historically hospitals tend to measure two broad outcomes: mortality and morbidity. **Mortality** is a measure of the rate of incidence for deaths, while **morbidity** is a measure of the rate of illness. These are good macro-level indicators that reflect long-term efforts, but they don't tell an organization much. These measures are too broad to really allow physicians and administrators to concentrate efforts on clinical improvements, and they also don't apply to other types of healthcare organizations.

So, many other more intermediate clinical outcomes and indicators that are linked to the broad metrics are now being used to better measure performance. Metrics such as frequency of medical errors and incorrect filling of pharmaceutical prescriptions are commonly utilized. There are many to choose from, as you will see.

Yet, healthcare involves more than clinical outcomes. All organizations are normally expected to be a "going concern" and therefore are expected to continue operations for the long term. This suggests survival, and to survive long term, organizations must have controls over financial results—such as cash flows, margins, debt, and working capital. **Key performance indicators** (KPI) are quantitative measures of performance used to evaluate the success that an organization has in meeting established objectives. There are organizational, strategic, and financial metrics. Financial KPIs for healthcare are shown in Table 11.1, and we will discuss these in much more detail in a subsequent chapter on analytics.

Financial results though are dictated by operations and strategy. Operationally, factors such as the number of personnel, productivity, investment of information technology, space, and facilities layout are all key to driving operational results. Strategically, organizations must focus on market share, growth rates, branding, and other key outcomes.

So, performance has multiple dimensions, all of which are important in different ways and times. Since performance improvement professionals are

Table 11.1   Key Financial Metrics

Financial Category	*Key Performance Indicator*
Profitability	• Operating margin • Profit margin • Earnings before interest, taxes, depreciation, amortization, and rent (EBITDA) • Return on assets • Return on equity
Debt Management	• Debt-equity ratio • Debt per bed (or discharge, adjusted patient day)
Efficiency	• Average payment period • Asset turnover • Inventory conversion ratio
Capital	• Net present value • Internal rate of return • Payback period

typically focused on "projects", the first task is to understand which aspect of performance to focus our efforts on. To do this, we need a framework for comprehensively understanding performance in healthcare.

Case 11.1: Orion Medical

Tom Spears heads up a for-profit group practice with just over 1,000 employees. When he joined the organization as President, he was faced with what he describes as a lack of comprehensive performance metrics. The only data that were commonly shared were business unit revenues, expenses, number of clinic visit, and patient volumes. Bringing together his senior team, he asked how these financial metrics connected to the planning framework and objectives. The organization's plan discussed strategic objectives and a stronger focus on patient satisfaction and new service line growth, but none of the KPIs were captured or shared internally. Even more disturbing was the lack of coordination with their key partners such as the local medical school and medical distributor. His solution was to refocus the KPIs around these stakeholders and the plan's strategic objectives immediately, and kick off a new planning session to address all strategic options more comprehensively.

Healthcare Strategy and Performance for Non-Profits

The performance of not-for-profit healthcare organizations is typically measured by the extent to which it achieved or contributed toward the mission and vision of the organization. Since most health systems and hospitals are not-for-profit, the mission is often stated in less financial terms and is more about serving the community, improving health outcomes, and increasing service and clinical quality.

Many not-for-profit organizations base their purpose and existence on a stated mission, usually defined in terms of meeting specific community needs. This makes it difficult to hold them accountable for performance related to mission because the specific metrics related to how well the mission is being fulfilled are often neglected or difficult to measure. The performance measures that organizations are generally held to are often "means" objectives, as opposed to the mission "ends". For example, mission often calls the organization to provide health services that improve community health status and enhance quality of life; however, typical performance measures for which management is held accountable are generally metrics such as profitability, return on investment, market share, and quality of care/service. Translating these to improvements in health status and quality of life might not be impossible but certainly challenging. So, the fundamental question is how does society, boards, and others hold organizations accountable for fulfilling their missions? How do we back into an assessment or judgment on how well management is doing with respect to mission and not just simply the "means" measures of performance. To that end, we should move toward more direct ways of measuring "mission performance" so that we can evaluate organizations and management in terms of how well they're doing with respect to their core purpose; i.e., the organization's mission. This will allow us to hold management and governance "accountable" for what they profess to be their purpose/mission. This is termed mission accountability (Langabeer, 2018; Sadhegi et al., 2012).

With regards to mission accountability, there are three dimensions that need to be measured:

1. How *much* an organization does toward their stated mission (measures of quantity),
2. How *well* an organization does it (one view of quality), and
3. How efficient the organization is at doing things (cost-effectiveness).

If we blend these three dimensions together (quantity, quality, and cost-effectiveness), we have a very good understanding of what healthcare organizations must do to survive and thrive today. Strategic performance therefore for most healthcare organizations is the sum of both mission performance and organizational performance, as shown below.

Performance Framework

In publicly traded industrial organizations, there is no dispute over goals and performance. Changes in market valuations and profitability (such as stock price, earnings per share, and economic value added) are the dominant outcomes. All decisions are taken (at least theoretically under rational conditions) to maximize these key integrative performance metrics. Since customer satisfaction, quality, and operations all need to be aligned to maximize one of these metrics, and since these firms are all attempting to maximize profits, they are very good metrics for understanding the organization's overall health. That works well in many industries.

Hospitals and health systems, however, are different for several reasons, which make it difficult to apply one singular metric:

1. Over 85% of all healthcare systems are not-for-profit in nature and seek to improve the public's health. If we tried to simply use financial performance as the outcome, this ignores a dominant mission.
2. Clinical and service quality often takes many years to become transparent to patients and payers. Although we are seeing many government agencies begin to push self-regulation and self-reporting of quality metrics, this is only in its infancy. Programs from both public and private organizations, such as the U.S. Department of Health and Human Services Agency for Healthcare Research and Quality (AHRQ), the Joint Commission, the National Association for Healthcare Quality, and the National Committee for Quality Assurance, are all making good strides toward quality reporting. Unfortunately, the transparency and visibility of this quality data meanwhile has a lower impact on current performance than in other industries.
3. Health systems are often required to take on charitable or indigent care, which obviously impacts financials significantly.
4. Healthcare organizations are investing aggressively in new medical technologies and research—which hopefully will pay off in terms of clinical outcomes in later years but often has a significantly negative impact on short-run performance.

Therefore, a useful performance framework for healthcare will integrate multiple aspects of financial performance.

The core dimensions of performance (i.e., quality, strategic, financial, operational) influence each other and are interrelated. If you make changes in some, they impact others, either positively or negatively. Also, the relative importance that each organization places on each dimension varies—some organizations focus most of their efforts on clinical quality, while some might be focused on financials or operations. This depends on several factors, such as their current state of affairs, the level of market turbulence, or the phase of the organization's life cycle. Finally, notice that there are quite a few variables or indicators in each performance dimension. There are probably quite a few more that are not listed, but these are the primary ones.

There needs to be a mechanism to allow managers to comprehensively understand the performance of their organization. Reports, financial statements, and other text-based assessments are often too time-consuming. What has emerged is the idea of a visual aid to see the key metrics for an organization.

One type of visual tool for managers is a balanced scorecard. **Balanced scorecard** is a set of measures that gives top managers a fast and comprehensive view of the organization's performance (Kaplan and Norton, 1992). The balanced scorecard recognizes that financial and operating metrics are always intertwined, so it is important to measure them simultaneously to understand their effects on each other and overall for the organization. This has also been applied in healthcare organizations for some time and has shown to provide significant benefits (Inamdar et al., 2002; Zelman et al., 2003). Use of a balanced scorecard in performance improvement will help to guide key measures and encourage alignment from one project team to another. Scorecards are also called dashboards.

For every project that a quality and performance improvement analyst undertakes, there *must* be a primary focus. At the planning stages, performance improvement analysts should identify which performance dimension this project is most likely to impact. The first stage of process improvement or project management starts with either a prioritization or **business case**, or the justification behind a project, but in many cases, the measures of improvement are very qualitative and intangible. These are sometimes referred to as soft benefits. Performance analysts should get to a deeper understanding of potential performance impacts prior to project kickoff, so that the project can be mapped out with this in mind. Unfortunately, many healthcare organizations ignore this stage and then question why they did not realize any benefits.

Absent defined performance criterion, quality coordinators should make their initial effort focused on defining performance dimensions, specific KPIs, and then ensuring that the project is developed and managed to eventually lead toward improvement in those areas.

Change versus Improvement

All projects that a performance improvement analyst undertake will have one of two forms: either they are exploratory or they are change-oriented. In many cases, however, even exploratory projects eventually become focused on change. **Change** is a transition from one state to another or a process of becoming different. Change is not always for the better good, but it is always different. Project professionals should *not* focus on achieving change for change's sake but rather to focus on making things better. **Improvement** is positive change or transition from something in a steady state to something better. Improvement adds value and delivers benefits in the expected performance dimension and specific key performance indicator.

As each project is undertaken, keeping the differences between change and improvement in mind is especially important. Projects, whether focused on process improvement or technology implementation, deliver change to people's work environments and processes. They may even impact their livelihood or that of their colleagues.

Improvement is relative. That is, improvement cannot become an absolute change across all projects for all measures. It must be defined in the initial project planning phase, with an understanding of where the existing performance is, what level of resources and investment will be made, and the timeframe provided. These three variables (current performance, resources, timeline) determine the relative improvements that can be made in any dimension.

Performance Management Basics

Performance improvement is tightly coupled with business strategy. Most healthcare organizations engage in a strategic planning process to develop a "strategy". As described in Chapter 1, strategy represents the direction and choice of a unique and valuable position rooted in systems of activities that are much more difficult to match (Porter, 1996). Alternatively, it is a path to move from where organizations are today, to where they want to be in the future. We will use the term strategy here synonymously with business strategy and organizational strategy. These are terms related to the highest levels of an organization, not single departments or functions. Both of these positions (current versus future) are measured in terms of performance, whether it is market share, clinical quality, patient satisfaction, or profitability. The mission of performance improvement therefore is to enable strategy.

The process of achieving a strategy in healthcare is rarely as simple as one giant leap in a specific area; rather, it is a collection of small improvements in a number of domains. In other words, if a hospital's primary strategy is to "improve brand and competitive position", then there might be a dozen or more initiatives which will have to be developed to achieve the strategy.

The process of setting performance objectives is typically one of the first processes in strategic planning. In many ways, professionals working on a project might have their performance targets dictated to them as a result of the strategic plans. In other environments, the plans simply serve as the framework for setting priorities and target areas.

Performance-Based Planning

Since all projects involve a focus on a specific outcome metric, then all projects need to essentially start by using a performance-driven planning approach. This requires the management analyst assemble the project team and clarify goals and objectives. Leading questions should be used, such as:

■ Where are we trying to go? Where are we moving from?
■ Which performance dimension are we the weakest in? Which ones are we strongest in?
■ What are our competition or benchmark organizations doing in this area? Are we behind them or leading them?
■ If we make a change in one performance area, will it impact others that we should be aware of?
■ How will these improvements impact patient satisfaction?
■ Do we really know our current performance levels?
■ Have we seen the measures graphically represented over time? Can we all agree on trends?

After these questions have thoroughly been explored, it becomes much easier to develop a common purpose for the project and to align the team around expectations and goals. This stage often takes considerable time, several hours per day for a week or longer—possibly more for really large projects such as an enterprise resource planning (ERP) or electronic health record (EHR) system implementation.

Once these high-level plans are initiated, the next step is to focus on performance specifics. These include asking questions, such as:

- What specific definition are we going to use for the metric? Although this may seem basic, it is necessary to apply a standardized and consistent definition to ensure comparability across other organizations and over time. The definition needs to be understood and embraced by all, so that it cannot be manipulated over the project to "ensure" project success.
- Where can we find existing data sources? What systems, either manual or electronic exist?
- If there are no existing sources of data, what investigational method will we use to measure current performance? (e.g., pilot project to identify process costs, observe waiting times, collect quality indicators).
- How long of a time period are we going to look back and forward? A minimum of 6 months pre and post is normally of sufficient length, but many projects wish to look 2 or 3 years out.

Notice that all of this planning comes before a specific method or tool is even discussed. One of the common problems is that a performance management analyst walks in the room with his "Six Sigma toolkit", or other methodology, but the first set of tasks is oriented not toward methods but toward discovery. **Discovery** is a thorough investigation of the present environment and collection of evidence. Discovery also requires that a thorough assessment be applied to understand performance relative to best practices and setting norms around the teamwork and project. Once the discovery occurs, a method can be applied based on the unique goals and challenges brought forth in the discovery. In essence, one tool or method cannot be applied to all projects.

One of the useful tools for discovery is the diagnostic assessment, which is created custom for each project. The assessment helps to quantitatively assess performance along a number of different process dimensions: personnel, technology, management systems, existing performance metrics, and many others. It requires the management engineer to do some initial work to help research and catalog best practices for the specific process or department, but it is invaluable to help prioritize work efforts and set the initial foundation.

Assessments such as these should be customized for each process and collectively evaluated by the group in order to provide project alignment and focus.

Goal Setting

We discussed in the leadership chapters about ambitious goals. The process of goal setting is very important for an organization. Within this framework, healthcare managers must find a way to define and align projects toward these performance dimensions, to enable the strategy. These could be automation and information systems, new building development, implementation of new service lines, or something entirely different. When the strategy has been established, the projects are defined, and the current performance levels are known, goals and objectives need to be established.

While these two terms—goals and objectives—are often used interchangeably, they are different. **Goals** are broad, long-term statements of an ideal future state. For instance, "the elimination of diabetes" is a very long-term goal. **Objectives** are more specific, short-term, quantifiable statements that are readily measurable. An example of an objective would be a "2.5% reduction in hospital acquired infection rates".

Goals and objectives help to transform the current performance level and path. With the introduction of a change (new project, system), the existing trend is shifted and results in new, hopefully more positive, improvements in performance levels.

While goals are typically broad and not easily measured on a periodic basis, objectives are. Objectives represent specific targets for managers and performance improvement analysts that should be tailored to individual projects. Setting performance targets is often difficult, however. If the project manager sets them too lofty, they are unachievable and might de-motivate staff and team members. If they are too easy, they deliver only marginal value for the organization. Achieving the right balance is very important. Certain goals should be "stretch" goals, which are harder to hit, encourage positive change, deliver substantial value, and motivate team members.

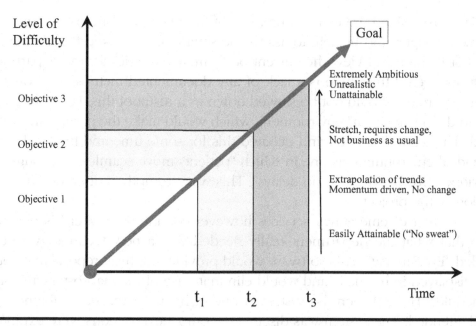

Figure 11.1   Setting strategic goals.

Figure 11.1 shows the differences between goals and objectives and how levels impact difficulty.

Also remember the guidelines discussed earlier. All performance targets must be measurable, quantifiable, consistent, and reliable indicators over time for that performance dimension.

Case 11.1: Hanes Hospital

A project has been undertaken by the emergency department (ED) at the Hanes Hospital, a large community hospital in urban Florida, to improve a key operational performance metric: "leave without being seen" (LWBS) rates. LWBS represents the number of times a patient left the ED without actually being seen by a healthcare provider. This is usually due to excessive wait times. The primary factor that initiated the project was patient complaints, and a concern by ED management that their current capacity was insufficient to handle their daily demand for accidents, trauma, and other emergencies.

Lucy Bobs was assigned the role of project manager. Lucy is an industrial engineer by training and is assigned to the Performance Solutions department. Lucy's manager informed her that the ED was especially "political" and influential, and that she needed to work very closely with them to ensure they remained satisfied.

Lucy assembled the team, comprised of the ED administrator, a surgeon, a nurse manager, and herself, to assess the situation. She asked the ED administrator if she could view the current performance metrics for the department and discovered that there is a lack of any documented metrics. She was told that the project should not be slowed down as a result of this. Lucy pushed to try to define an "ideal" environment, which would make the participants satisfied. The team discussed and debated this for some time and finally defined the ideal environment as one in which "patients move seamlessly through the perioperative period with no delays". This was promptly written down as the vision of the project.

The chief of emergency services however continued to offer his perspective that what the department really needed was a new technology system called "ED Fantasy". This software would provide graphical reports that could be displayed in the halls and would eliminate use of manual rosters and shift schedules. He had seen the system at one of his most recent conferences he had attended. The system was discussed, competitive options were explored, and then the vendor was called for pricing.

Soon thereafter, the purchasing department was contacted to put a request for proposal (RFP) out on the street, and after 60 more days, a license agreement was in place. Implementation started soon after, and "ED Fantasy" went live nearly 180 days after that.

Following completion of the project, Lucy was asked to write a summary document that described the success of the project. She described the project as having a total duration of 250 days (well under the 365-day average project duration), rapid implementation of new technology, and satisfied ED stakeholders. Overall, Lucy considered this a very successful project.

In this case study, the performance analyst did a reasonably good job in many respects: she obviously helped to keep momentum in the team, helped achieve some level of perceived success, and kept the team intact, which is sometimes quite a feat. However, there are also many lessons we can learn about what Lucy failed to do properly. She failed to perform any benchmarking, she allowed the primary sponsor to direct the efforts solely toward a technology solution, and she viewed the project too narrowly in terms of expectations. All these can be overcome by following the guidelines and suggestions offered below.

Benchmarking

One way to establish benefit or performance targets is to benchmark against other hospitals or health systems. **Benchmarking** is the comparison of a key performance measurement relative to the competition or other leading organizations. It can also be defined as the process of seeking best practices among better performing organizations, with intentions of applying those internally.

There are a number of different types of benchmarking—those that focus on process, services, best practices, or competition. In most respects however, the purpose is the same (to compare and assess), but their specific focus or unit of analysis is different. For example, suppose that there are five hospitals in the same large, urban city. The Chief Nursing Officer hired a performance engineer to help analyze how overall nursing productivity (measured as # of total procedures performed divided by the nursing labor time) compares to the other four organizations. At a high level, the analyst could simply look up the labor and volume data historically, using secondary published data available from the American Hospital Directory or the American Hospital Association. Doing this provides a baseline comparison that can be analyzed over time to get trends. This would be a good example of competitive benchmarking, where the best practice organizations can be identified and further reviewed. If the analyst was to call the other sites, ask for a walk-through of the floors or units, and observe the functions in detail, this is a good example of process benchmarking.

There are both limitations and advantages to using primary and secondary data in benchmarking. Obviously, direct interviews and observations are typically better than using secondary data in some respects, since the data is more real time and allows for feedback and communication about definitions and metrics. Primary data however also have their own limitations, such as the interviewee giving biased or skewed responses, based on their interpretations of questions, or simply wanting to make their process seem superior to others.

Probably, the best way we've found to collect performance benchmarking data is to use best practice organizations in other cities, to avoid competitive concerns about sharing of data. The process is fairly straight forward, with five steps: identify problems and gaps, identify best practice organizations, prepare for visit, conduct site visit, and adopt practices into organization.

Identify Problems and Gaps

Identify the specific problem area, whether it is a process concern or a performance gap. Then, clearly document the problem and define the current process capabilities. Process capabilities include analysis of the historical data and trends, and the use of capability index (such as C_{pk}, described in the next chapter), using statistical analyses of the transactional or performance data if at all possible.

Research and Identify Best Practice Organizations

Conduct a search, using published data or library searches of those organizations that appear to have best practice. Ideally, these should be the organizations that have established themselves as the leader in the specific area you are focusing on. The use of newsletters, journals, magazines, or case studies is often one way to find these best practices. Once identified, the organization should be contacted and a site visit requested. Other potential resources for data include the following associations, organizations, and agencies:

1. Healthcare Information and Management Systems Society (www.himss.org)
2. American College of Healthcare Executives (www.ache.org)
3. Healthcare Financial Management Association (www.hfma.org)
4. American Medical Informatics Association (www.amia.org)
5. National Quality Forum (www.qualityforum.org)
6. Agency for Healthcare Research and Quality (www.ahrq.gov)
7. National Association for Healthcare Quality (www.nahq.org)
8. National Committee for Quality Assurance (www.ncqa.org)
9. Centers for Medicare and Medicaid Services (www.cms.hhs.gov)
10. Joint Commission (www.jointcommission.org)
11. DNV Healthcare (http://dnvglhealthcare.com)
12. American Hospital Directory (www.ahd.com)
13. American Hospital Association (www.aha.org)
14. ProQuest ABI/Inform (www.proquest.com)
15. National Institute for Health and Excellence, UK (www.nice.org.uk)

Prepare for Benchmarking Visit

Prepare detailed plans for what you hope to gain from the visit. Preparation is key and is often minimized. Adequate preparation ensures that a full set of questions are developed, a plan for how to spend the time with the host is constructed and shared, and both parties understand the goals and objectives for the visit. Showing up a benchmarking site with no plan is a waste of a lot of resources. Questions will obviously vary by site and by process. For an evaluation of a new information system, where best practices of the implementation are to be analyzed, some generic questions could include the following listed in Table 11.2.

Conduct Site Visit

The next step is to conduct the actual site visit. This is when the preparation from the previous step will be executed. It is important to bring the right people to the visit, and assign people to take detailed notes and collect any documentation necessary for follow-up. During the visit, observing first-hand

Table 11.2 Potential Benchmarking Visit Questions

1. What was the projected benefit versus amount realized? What was the primary reason for the variances?
2. Which one system or process drives most of the business value?
3. What is an estimate of the total cost of this project or system? How much of this was planned versus unexpected?
4. What are some of your biggest lessons learned?
5. If you could do it over again, what would you do differently?
6. What are you least proud of in the implementations?
7. Which task on the project timeline took significantly more resources or time than you estimated? How many people were involved in the overall project? How many were dedicated 100%?
8. Which vendors did you select? Why were they chosen?
9. What was the total project timeline? Was it far off from the original projection?
10. What was the overall reaction by your staff in the beginning (e.g., positive, negative, indifferent)? Why?
11. What were the three greatest improvements in actual performance indicators or process capabilities?
12. Were there any technical or system glitches we should be aware of?
13. What surprises did you encounter?
14. What role did consultants play in this process?
15. Can we see an example of the system?
16. Do you have any performance scorecards we could look at?

the participants, events, activities, and systems in the process being reviewed is critical, in addition to getting all the questions addressed that help you to understand the best practice and adopt it post-benchmarking.

Adopt and Integrate Best Practices

Post-visit, it is important to gather the benchmarking team, discuss findings, document the best practices, and most importantly, incorporate these into the plans and process changes immediately. Adapting the best practices, and adopting them into your own, is the only way that benchmarking proves to be a valuable exercise.

Guidelines for Performance Management

Achieving improvement is difficult, even in the best of conditions. Below are guidelines or recommendations for how performance improvement consultants can use their project to deliver value to the organization: define success carefully, measure historical performance, forecast desired improvement target, and believe you are the expert.

Define Success More Carefully

One of the most common problems in process improvement work is that the initial task of defining desired performance is often cut short. Administrators in healthcare tend to believe they already know the problem that exists and where they want to go, without any careful analysis or discovery of facts. More than any other industry, healthcare also tends to define performance very abstractly and broadly, which makes it easy to claim success in post-project evaluations, but very difficult to prove.

The initial effort in this case study needed to select a performance dimension and associated set of KPIs right from the beginning. Collaboratively, the group needed to spend the appropriate amount of time brainstorming and planning desired performance impacts: would a project impact quality, financials, operations, or a combination? Which specific metric? In many cases, there has been virtually no planning around performance indicators, and so when a project for technology or process is initiated, the first step has to be to carefully plan! It is easy to skip this step, but then really all that a project can really claim is that they delivered change, not improvement.

Measure Historical Performance

Once the team identified or developed the ideal performance criteria, there needed to be effort to develop a methodology for collecting and analyzing the data behind that indicator. For example, assume it was waiting times for patients. Without an understanding of current levels of wait periods, how can an organization suggest that any improvements were made post-project? However, that is what happens in many cases: organizations suggest that they don't have the right system or process in place to measure current results, so only after the project is successful can they begin to measure. That is flawed thinking.

In industrial organizations, only those projects are undertaken which deliver results. To prove results, one must measure the delta, or change, between pre- and post-project metrics. This thinking has to become more customary in healthcare if real improvements are to be made. Industrial engineers, project managers, and performance improvement professionals all play a pivotal role in helping make this a reality.

Forecast Desired Improvement Target

Once the performance indicator is established, and historical data is collected, a target must be created to show desired direction and level for that criterion. If it is waiting times, and historically the OR showed 1.6 hours of wait pre-surgery, then the project needs to make a reasonable target for future performance. Ideally, this should be staged based on timing. For example, "in the first six months post-project, wait times will decrease 30% to 67 minutes". That way, the desired performance target is:

- *Measurable*, in both absolute and relative terms,
- *Quantitative*, using precise percentage changes numerically,
- *Consistent*, with existing definition and data over multiple periods, and
- *Relevant*, by using the right performance dimension.

Don't Let Benefits Leak Out

Performance gains do accrue to successful projects, but even those that are meticulously planned and executed have some benefit leakage. According to Mankins and Steele (2005), only 63% of the total potential performance gains are realized by most organizations. Performance losses occur because of inadequate resources, poor strategy, lack of accountability, lack of monitoring, and many other reasons. Using the right methods, for the right project, and maintaining a perspective focused on pre- and post-performance is key to maintaining those performance gains over the long term.

Chapter Summary

- The quest for operational excellence comes from performance management techniques.
- Healthcare performance is complex and multi-dimensional. Performance is much more than just financial results in most health systems.
- Strategy and performance analysts are often tasked with both implementation and performance improvement.
- Alignment is key to ensuring that post-implementation, performance is managed effectively.

Discussion Questions

1. What are the core components of performance management?
2. How does your organization's strategy impact the type of performance improvement projects you work on?
3. What level of difficulty should you use when setting goals and objectives?
4. Which type of performance indicator do you feel is the most important in healthcare?

Key Terms

Balanced Scorecard; Benchmarking; Change; Discovery; Goals; Improvement; Key Performance Indicator; Mortality; Morbidity; Objectives; Operational Excellence; Performance Management

References

Inamdar N, Kaplan RS, and Bower M (2002). Applying the balanced scorecard in healthcare provider organizations. *Journal of Healthcare Management, 47*(3), 195–196.

Kaplan RS and Norton D (1992). The balanced scorecard: measures that drive performance. *Harvard Business Review, 70*(1), 71–79.

Langabeer J (2018). *Performance Improvement in Hospitals and Health Systems* (2nd ed). Chicago, IL: Routledge Press.

Langabeer J and Helton J (2020). *Healthcare Operations Management: A Systems Perspective*, 3rd Edition. Boston, MA: Jones and Bartlett Publishers.

Mankins MC and Steele R (2005). Turning great strategy into great performance. *Harvard Business Review, 83*(8), 64–72.

Porter M (1996). What is strategy? *Harvard Business Review*, November–December.

Sadhegi S, Barsi A, Mikhail O, and Shabot M (2012). *Integrating Quality and Strategy in Health Care Organizations*. Boston, MA: Jones and Bartlett Publishers.

Zelman W, Pink G, and Matthias C (2003). Use of the balanced scorecard in healthcare. *Journal of Healthcare Finance, 29*(4), 1–16.

Chapter 12

Managing Organizational Quality

Introduction

Quality is defined both internally (did we meet specifications?) and externally (did our customers and patients receive the value they expected?). Quality management philosophy guides all performance improvement for an organization. Performance improvement is essentially about changing results for an organization, whether that is a clinic, hospital, surgical center, health department, insurance company, or healthcare delivery system. Implied in this are changes to both the inputs and the process that produce those outcomes. There is generally ambiguity about definitions and differences between process improvement, performance improvement, and quality improvement, and many other terms. In this chapter, we will review the theories and concepts underlying quality management and performance improvement.

Quality

You might remember that prior to the year 2000, the American car industry was heading toward disaster. Quality—in the eyes of the consumers who purchased and drove these vehicles—was gauged to be extremely low and sales declined to such a point that countries such as Japan and Germany were thought to be the only places to find quality. Some US makers had even

DOI: 10.4324/9781032623726-15

declared bankruptcy. Competitiveness of American car manufacturers was limited. But then the American car industry rebounded and now tops many of the consumer quality ratings for different car types. At the same time, other countries such as South Korea have also emerged as leaders. What happened? Changes in design, manufacturing, and service. In short, process and quality improvement allowed companies to focus on consumer needs.

Similarly, the healthcare industry is trying to rebound from its own crisis. The landmark report by the National Academy of Medicine (formerly the Institute of Medicine) called "To Err Is Human" helped to create a national awareness of the significant quality and safety issue surrounding health (Kohn et al., 2000). The report estimated that between 44,000 and 98,000 people die every year from preventable accidents and errors in hospitals. The combined costs of these deaths and other quality issues could amount to up to $29 billion each year alone.

We will start with a basic definition for quality. **Quality** is a perception of the level of value a customer places on an organization's outputs, and the degree to which these meet established specifications and benchmarks. Everything an organization does impacts quality, from the type of furniture to the recruitment of employees. Quality is reflected at both the institutional level (e.g., overall number of medical errors) and at the process/departmental level (e.g., aspirins administered on cardiac patients).

Even the use of basic information technologies, such as the electronic health record (I), create potential quality concerns. An **electronic health record** is a comprehensive longitudinal electronic record that stores patient health data in a hospital or clinic, including patient demographics, prior medical history, interventions performed, laboratory and test results, medications, and many other types of data.

Sittig and Singh (2012) point out that information systems have a significant impact on quality, including: miscommunication between providers, system downtime and access issues that impact patients, "alert fatigue" where providers override system messages, and many other quality concerns resulting from failure to adopt and implement new systems properly.

Aside from clinical quality and outcomes, there are issues with regards to quality of business and administrative processes. There is an extremely high amount of inefficiency and administrative waste, in everything from revenue cycle to supply chain management. Prominent researchers have claimed that nearly $1 trillion in wasteful spending occurs because of administrative complexity, process failures, fraud and abuse, overtreatment, and overspending, among others (Sahni et al., 2015; Berwick and Hackbarth, 2012).

Quality costs can be high. **Cost of quality** represents the sum of all costs associated with providing inferior, error-prone, or poor-quality services. Some of these are avoidable costs of failure, defects, and errors (example would be surgery on the wrong body part, or an avoidable hospital readmission). Other costs are necessary, such as the cost of preventing errors (such as checklists and protocols). Then, there are the opportunity costs of what your organization could have done with the resources that went into poor quality and rework. Cost of quality is the sum of all costs to avoid, prevent, and provide inferior services.

Cleary, quality is a major concern. Improving quality and performance needs to be taken seriously. The term quality conjures up a lot of different definitions. Despite lots of attention, there is still ambiguity surrounding the precise meaning of quality (Reeves and Bednar, 1994). Quality can be defined by multiple dimensions, including the following:

- *Customer.* Customers pay the bills, so this definition suggests that meeting and exceeding the customer's expectations is a requirement for quality. Of course, in healthcare, the term customer is also confusing, since we have a separation between the consumer of the service and the payer in many respects. Regardless, many marketing and management scholars over the years have thought that organizations should deliver what the customer wants and needs, and that if they meet those expectations, then the products will sell and the company will grow (Buzzell and Gale, 1987; Deming, 1986). This is one of the most important definitions for quality in healthcare.
- *Value.* Quality is often seen as equal to value produced in terms of total outcomes in relationship to their costs. Dr. Michael Porter, a leading scholar from the Harvard Business School, suggests that this definition is the most applicable to healthcare (Porter, 2010). It makes sense, because everything we do to improve quality should be considered relative to its cost. If we add ten patient rooms to reduce wait times, does that change in service levels offset by higher costs that cannot be recovered? **Value** in healthcare is an expression of the relationship between outcomes produced by an organization and costs over time.
- *Fitness for Use.* The term "fitness for use" was created by Joseph Juran, to indicate that the product or service should do what it is intended to do. Users (customers) should be able to count on it to do what it is supposed to do (Juran, 1992). In healthcare, this would suggest that customers intend for our physicians diagnoses and treatments to be correct

and to help heal us. Waiting rooms should be comfortable enough, technology should support the process, and staff should be trained appropriately. All of these suggest fitness for use.

- *Conformance.* Quality is often viewed in terms of how well it meets or conforms to the specifications or the requirements for the product or service (Crosby, 1979). This definition cares less about how the customer views it, but whether it was delivered as designed. This definition seems to work well in some areas, such as manufacturing. In terms of healthcare, it isn't widely applied.
- *Excellence.* Quality has been defined as the pursuit of the highest standards and results and not settling for average or typical outcomes (Peters and Waterman, 1984). We see this when we look at specific institutions which seem to strive for excellence daily. Certain health systems are continually innovating and excelling. But, this definition cannot be for everybody, since excellence does have a cost. Or can it?

So, is quality conformance to a specification? Excellence? Meeting or exceeding customer's expectations? Achieving value? It's these things, or maybe a mix of them, depending on your own organization's strategy and beliefs. How do you currently perceive your organization's quality relative to others? Analysts should always first examine how leadership in their organization enables and operationalizes quality. What is being discussed at organizational staff meetings? What are the primary drivers of concern?

Quality can be defined in different ways, making performance improvement more difficult. It is essential to understand how your organization defines and implements quality into their strategy to focus on improvements.

Delivery organizations should make sure they include aspects of patient satisfaction, health, and safety outcomes relative to costs (value) and adherence to the latest clinical evidence. **Evidence** is empirical data, or proof, supporting a decision or position. Health and safety outcomes in this case should be both prevention (preventable readmissions or acquired infections for example) and clinical process of care (compliance with guideline-based aspirin or medication interventions). It is vital that your own organization ensure that they agree on how they wish to define quality and align that with internal staff and stakeholders. To change quality, there must be alignment in the organization. A quality management approach should drive your performance improvement efforts.

Quality Management

Quality management is a management philosophy focused on systematically improving performance and processes (Deming, 1986; Dean and Bowen, 1994). Quality management is necessary to guide business and clinical performance improvement and to achieve organizational competitiveness. **Competitiveness** is the ability of an organization to provide goods and services that are superior to rivals and produces value for customers and long-term sustainability. If done correctly, this involves assumptions and principles that flow through the organization, resulting in changes to culture and beliefs in the leadership and employees. Culture refers to core values and beliefs shared by all employees and management in an organization. A commitment to quality helps organizations strive for better results continuously over time. It suggests a relentless pursuit of positive change on outcomes, efficiency, and overall outcomes.

Improving quality is necessary to achieve better results, and a high-quality strategy can produce significant gains in strategic measures, such as market share, profitability, and overall competitiveness (Buzzell and Gale, 1987). It can also significantly reduce medical and medication errors, improve patient safety, and drive other meaningful improvements in clinical care. In this era of heightened competition, the edge gained from better quality is vital.

A quality management approach embeds many different foci, and we will discuss these throughout the book. But, at a minimum, the formula driving quality management includes these components: competitive strategy, organizational culture and teamwork, customer focus, and performance management systems.

A strategy should commit the organization to achieving superior quality and improving perceived quality by customers (patients). Strategy sets the organizational direction and provides details on how the vision will be enabled. We focus more on this in the subsequent chapter. Strategy requires solid leadership, focused on doing things right and doing the right things. Leaders in high-quality health organizations provide direction that enables employees to make the right decisions fixated on customers, outcomes, costs, and value. Strategy and leadership are interconnected.

In addition, successful hospitals and health systems should adopt a long-term horizon and organizational culture that rewards improvements and continuously changes through systemic process modeling that weeds out waste and improves outcomes. Culture is difficult to change, especially in more mature and established organizations, but recognition of efforts and rewards for process changes helps to stimulate a quality culture. Teamwork is an important aspect of culture. Teamwork fosters internal partnerships and collaboration between different people and departments to achieve results.

Importantly, there must be a focus on customers, both external and internal. Customer focus helps to improve transparency and provide services that customers really want and need. The culture needs to support the emphasis on external customers and partners, as well as internal staff and physicians.

Finally, organizations need to adopt a methodology for improvement and use of tools and techniques. Throughout this book, we will describe several of them, but most basic methods require an approach to defining and structuring a problem, measuring current performance, setting goals, making process changes, and continuously improving and refining. Methodologies such as Six Sigma, Lean, or PDCA are similar in many respects but differ in others. Regardless of the chosen methodology, analysts should make use of tools and techniques, such as forecasting, predictive modeling, and simulation.

Core Components of Quality Management

There are many different beliefs and principles of quality management that have been identified over time by different researchers, including Shewhart, Deming, Juran, Crosby, and many others. We will describe a few of the contributions from the early leaders in the field.

Dr. Walter Shewhart (an engineer and physicist) was the first researcher to describe the need for and methods used in quality control. Shewhart published landmark texts on this field in the early 1930s, influencing the next three quality gurus after him who began in the 1950s. Shewhart is best known as the founder of the plan, do, check, act (PDCA) cycle which is in extensive use today as the dominant methodology in healthcare organizations.

Dr. W. Edwards Deming (an engineer and statistician) helped to create a philosophy of management which uses statistical analysis to reduce variation or variability in processes and outcomes. **Variability** refers to the relative degree of dispersion of data points, especially as they differ from the norm. Deming created control charts and other tools that continue in use today. He strongly believed that management needs to embrace a culture focused on continuous improvement for any change to be successful. This included a focus on long-term profits, constancy of organizational purpose, and stability in management, among others, which he defined in his "fourteen points" and "seven deadly diseases" (Deming, 2000).

Dr. Joseph Juran (an engineer and consultant) also believed that quality improvement should be integrated into management theory. He was the first to apply the Pareto principle to quality. Pareto principle states that 80% of a problem can be attributed to 20% of the cause. He advocated the use of a **Pareto Chart**, which is a combination bar/line graph depicting individual and cumulative frequency represented in descending order. The frequency or outcome is shown on the Y axis, and the reasons or causes for that are shown on the X axis. He also developed the three phases of quality management (planning, control, and improvement), which we will describe further in the next section. These phases are critical to the belief that quality improvements lead to long-term performance improvements (Juran, 1989).

Mr. Philip B. Crosby (a quality manager) was the first to state that "zero defects" or error-free production should be the norm and not the exception. **Zero defect** is a philosophy that expects managers to prevent errors before they begin, which reduces total costs by doing things right the first time (Crosby, 1979). As stated in his book, Crosby believed that "quality is free", implying that prevention of errors will pay for itself in the long run.

Of course, there are others who made significant contributions. Dr. Genichi Taguchi emphasized designing in quality the first time. Dr. Kaoru Ishikawa created the concept of a cause-and-effect diagram (now called "fishbone" diagrams). There are many others from the field of quality, statistics, and management that all had influences on quality and performance improvement. Although all had unique contributions, they seemingly agree in a few common areas. Table 12.1 summarizes the key principles of quality.

Table 12.1 Quality Principles

- Quality can only be achieved by continuous measurement and focus.
- Decision-making should be driven by data.
- Performance gains will be realized when the organization is committed to it.
- The people that do the work are best positioned to improve upon it.
- Teamwork is essential.
- A systems orientation ensures that organizations don't optimize one process which negatively impacts the whole.

Planning, Control, and Improvement

Juran described three primary phases in improving performance and quality: planning, improvement, and control. Together these activities raise the performance levels for organizations. Later we will discuss how these are integrated in the common performance improvement methodologies, such as PDCA or Six Sigma. Figure 12.1 shows the improvement cycle.

Planning for quality and performance involves addressing the issue of how your organization defines quality. Fundamentally, this entails defining whether that means "patient satisfaction" or "conformance to requirements" or "value". Once it is understood, and leadership shares this and creates a common culture around it, then planning should address how to ensure that this is met. The planning process should adopt specific methodologies for how performance will be improved and embrace the tools and techniques that will be used across the institution. These tools might include flowcharting, benchmarking, statistical sampling, customer satisfaction surveys, and many others which will be discussed in subsequent chapters.

Improvement includes the activities necessary to ensure that your organization is following the standards and requirements that were established in the planning phase. Improvement involves making changes to processes that work toward desired goals. There are several different methods and analytics we use to improve processes.

Control processes ensure that we meet quality standards and tend to be the primary focus of continuous improvement. **Statistical process control** (SPC) is the term used for applying statistics to monitor and control

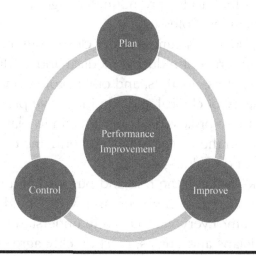

Figure 12.1   Improvement cycle.

the behavior of a process. Routine audits of performance are typically conducted, as well as process analysis using flowcharts, cause-and-effect diagrams, histograms, and other visualizations to bring processes to desired levels.

Need for Healthcare Improvement

As we approach the year 2020, there is a greater need for change and improvement than ever before, especially in healthcare. The term **Kaizen** is the Japanese word for continuous improvement. Kaizen should be the standard practice in healthcare. Medical costs continue to grow at rates nearly triple that of other industries, despite technology and other efforts to curb their growth. Health outcomes, quality, and cost-effectiveness of healthcare processes have become center stage for every hospital or healthcare system. US healthcare expenditures in 2009 were just $2 trillion annually (4 times the national defense budget, or about $7,500 per person). In 2020, the Centers for Medicare and Medicaid Services project it to be around $4.2 trillion, or $12,500 per capita (CMS, 2017). That rate of growth in costs over a decade is phenomenal and unsustainable.

A big part of this expense is purely waste. Waste in terms of duplication of effort, over-utilization of resources, and inefficient administration and clinical processes. While federal government and macro-level policy change might bring change in the long term, in the near term, change must come from within organizations. Who do these organizations—the hospitals, clinics, and systems—look to for promoting change internally? Quality and performance improvement professionals.

At the same time, quality of care is under close examination. Organizations can do much better in terms of reducing medical and medication errors. That is the role of administrators, analysts, and other professionals—to enhance the performance and quality of clinical and administrative processes. As process and system experts, these professionals must begin to play a broader role in re-defining healthcare in the United States and bringing cost-effective healthcare to our hospitals and health systems.

So, you might ask—what is the role and purpose of a quality improvement manager or management engineer, and why should healthcare organizations invest in them? Everyone intuitively understands why clinics and hospitals need physicians and nurses; most quickly agree that as technology becomes more integrated and essential to patient care that IT professionals are necessary, but only a small minority fully understand and appreciate the full potential of professionals dedicated to improving the performance of management systems, workflow, and outcomes. Yet, the value and contribution of the professionals that dedicate their efforts to performance and process improvement daily is substantial.

Industrial engineering techniques have been applied to healthcare since the early 1900s. While industrial engineers such as Frank and Lillian Gilbreth focused on process efficiency, others such as Frederick Taylor worked on improving productivity using time and motion studies. Together, these early pioneers showed surgeons and providers that the healthcare industry could benefit from process improvement much the same as manufacturing industries (Heineke and Davis, 2007). This is evident in efforts to redesign the clinician's workflow to increase outputs in the operating room as an example. The field was significantly advanced by Harold Smalley, one of the founding fathers of the Healthcare Management Systems Society—which later became the Healthcare Information and Management Systems Society. Since this time, we have seen growth in the number of organizations, journals, and training opportunities in the "science of improvement", but it is still insufficient. We need greater penetration of employees focused on attacking the obstacles and roadblocks facing healthcare and using a combination of engineering and organizational development techniques.

Performance Improvement

Quality management (QM) professionals focus on improving quality and performance. **Performance improvement**, sometimes called process improvement, is an approach that analyzes, measures, and changes business and clinical processes to improve outcomes. Performance improvement involves establishing better management systems. **Management systems** are the framework of all processes, policies, procedures, standards, and other documentation that defines how an organization should behave in order to achieve their purpose. Management systems outline the work environment that must be conducted to execute daily operations. **Performance** reflects the inputs, process, and outcomes (results) for specific areas. Performance improvement analysts apply engineering, statistical, and analytical techniques to understand the behavior or processes and then work with teams to create recommendations for process change.

Historically in healthcare, a small group of quantitatively trained professionals were considered healthcare engineers, focused on making improvements in processes and systems. This specialty became known as **management engineering**, which is the application of engineering principles to healthcare processes. It focuses on designing optimal management and information systems and processes, using tools from engineering, mathematics, and social sciences.

Most commonly, performance improvement approaches start with analysis of the behavior of processes using a framework that ensures that decisions are analytical and data-driven. We tend to express variables and activities in quantitative terms, using actual data obtained from information systems or calculated from observations. This mapping of process behavior and modeling in statistical ways is essential to identify areas for improvement and then measure the effects of change.

This often resembles a mathematical or engineering approach, where science is applied to decisions. This approach supports data-driven management. **Data-driven management** is the use of proven and established organizational practices to improve decisions and results (Langabeer and Helton, 2020; Walshe and Rundall, 2001). Data-driven management suggests that data drives decisions, not just assumptions and intuitions. This requires a systems orientation. **Systems orientation** understands that all activities and processes are interconnected, and that change in one produces change elsewhere. This is not just referring to "information" systems but management and organizational systems and the activities for the healthcare ecosystem. A policy for evaluating employees, for example, is a management system. So too are procedures for handling patient complaints.

Performance improvement incorporates cost-effectiveness as well, by understanding not just results but the relationships between incremental value produced from a process and its associated costs. As described earlier, value in healthcare is an expression of the relationship between outcomes produced by an organization and costs over time. Since most gains in performance come only through additional expenses (such as investing in new technology or equipment), quality analysts can help play a valuable role in identifying useful practices that have high cost-effectiveness, thereby ensuring resources are applied optimally.

There are a number of areas to focus on and a number of different job titles and roles in organizations that help in performance improvement. These roles and focus are shown in Table 12.2.

Table 12.2   Roles and Focus of Performance Improvement Team

Functional Title	Focus
Quality Manager	Mapping process behavior
Quality Coordinator	Data analysis and modeling
Process Consultant	Leading work teams
Business Process Analyst	Implementing change
Project Manager	Managing projects
Management Engineer/Analyst	Developing systems orientation, improving outcomes
Operations Analyst	Mapping process behavior
Strategy Analyst	Incorporating intelligence, strategy alignment

While quality and performance professionals in the past can best be classified as "tacticians" or "technicians", today's analysts are agents of change. They are internal consultants that help executives better manage projects; they are leaders of key IT and capital projects; they use collaboration and facilitation skills to guide team efforts; and they understand performance drivers and technology better than anyone in the organization to help make changes stick. Performance improvement has become an issue for the boardroom, and now is the time for engineers and analysts to expand their toolkit and take a visible, leadership role in organizational change.

The breadth and scope of performance improvement and quality management professionals is growing. Analysts and quality coordinators can get involved in a variety of different activities and projects. Examples of these are shown in Table 12.3.

Table 12.3   Types of Quality and Performance Improvement Activities

Implementation of systems and technology	New facility construction projects
Development of business plans	Process workflow redesign
Performance benchmarking	Productivity and staffing management
Supply chain re-engineering	Simulation modeling of clinics and units
Cataloging and deploying evidence to improve medical quality	Data mining for decision-making

Summary

Quality is measured in multiple ways but is gauged by customers' perceptions and the value (outcomes relative to costs) delivered by the organization. Quality management is a philosophy that systematically improves long-term quality and performance improvement. There are multiple pillars of quality management, including strategy and leadership; measurement and improvement activities; culture and teamwork; and a strong commitment to the customer. Three key activities drive Kaizen (continuous improvement): planning, improvement, and control. Performance improvement are those efforts geared to delivering improved results and outcomes, with full awareness of the impact on overall costs and resource utilization.

Discussion Questions

1. How competitive do you think most hospitals are today?
2. What does quality mean to you? To your organization?
3. As a healthcare consumer, do you believe you can objectively find quality measures on your physicians and hospitals? Why or why not?
4. If you were the CEO, what would you do differently to ensure higher quality?
5. Will the concept of zero defects ever be a reality in healthcare?

Key Terms

Competitiveness; Cost of Quality; Culture; Electronic Health Record; Evidence; Data-Driven Management; Kaizen; Management Engineering; Management Systems; Pareto Chart; Performance; Performance Improvement; Statistical Process Control; Strategy; Systems Orientation; Quality; Quality Management; Value; Variability; Zero Defects

References

Berwick D and Hackbarth A (2012). Eliminating waste in US health care. *Journal of the American Medical Association* (JAMA), *307*(14), 1513–1516.

Buzzell R and Gale B (1987). *The Profit Impact of Marketing Strategy: Linking Strategy to Performance.* New York: The Free Press.

Centers for Medicare and Medicaid Services (CMS) (2017). CMS, office of the actuary. *National Health Expenditures*, 2016–2025 Forecast Summary. Available at www.cms.gov

Crosby P (1979). *Quality is Free: The Art of Making Quality Certain*. New York: New American Library.

Dean J and Bowen D (1994). Managing theory and total quality: improving research and practice through theory development. *Academy of Management Review*, *19*(3), 392–418.

Deming WE (1986). *Quality, Productivity, and Competitive Position*. Cambridge, MA: Massachusetts Institute of Technology Center for Advanced Engineering Study.

Deming WE (2000). *Out of the Crisis*. Cambridge, MA: MIT Press.

Heineke J and Davis M (2007). The emergence of service operations management as an academic discipline. *Journal of Operations Management*, *25*(2), 364–374.

Juran JM (1989). *Juran on Leadership for Quality*. New York: Free Press.

Juran JM (1992). *Juran on Quality by Design: The New Steps for Planning Quality into Goods and Services*. New York: Free Press.

Kohn LT, Corrigan JM, and Donaldson MS eds. (2000). *To Err is Human: Building a Safer Health System*. National Academy of Medicine. Washington, DC: National Academies Press.

Langabeer J and Helton J (2020). *Healthcare Operations Management: A Systems Perspective*, 3rd Edition. Boston, MA: Jones and Bartlett Publishers.

Peters T and Waterman R (1984). *In Search of Excellence: Lessons from America's Best-Run Companies*. New York: Grand Central Publishing.

Porter M (2010). What is value in health care? *New England Journal of Medicine*, *363*, 2477–2481.

Reeves C and Bednar D (1994). Defining quality: alternatives and implications. *Academy of Management Review*, *19*(3), 419–445.

Sahni N, Chigurupati A, Kocher B, and Cutler D (2015). How the U.S. can reduce healthcare spending by $1 Trillion. *Harvard Business Review*, October 13, 2015.

Sittig D and Singh H (2012). Electronic health records and national patient-safety goals. *New England Journal of Medicine*, *367*, 1854–1860.

Walshe K and Rundall TG (2001). Evidence-based management: from theory to practice in health care. *Milbank Quarterly*, *79*,429–457.

Chapter 13

Continuous Performance Improvement

Introduction

Successful organizations continue to learn from their prior experiences, and have an inclination towards continuous performance improvement. The choice of which performance management methodology to adopt is a critical one. Multiple methods exist, from PDCA to Six Sigma, Lean, and Theory of Constraints to name just a few. Each method has its own goal, tools, and approach. In this chapter, we will explore the methodologies and the tools and techniques underlying these methods.

Quality Measures

Dr. Avedis Donabedian (a physician and quality outcomes pioneer) created a conceptual model that defines how healthcare outcomes and performance can be improved (Donabedian, 2005). The **Donabedian model** is a structural framework for examining quality of care (Figure 13.1).

As shown in the figure, this model implies that the inputs (or underlying structure of an organization and its environment) determine how providers and administrators in an organization will act. Structure includes all types of resources, such as facilities, technology and systems, finances, and personnel, among others.

DOI: 10.4324/9781032623726-16

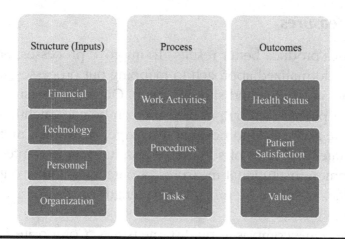

Figure 13.1 The Donabedian model.

The Donabedian model helped to frame quality and performance outcomes in healthcare. Consequently, there are different types of measures for structure, process, and outcomes.

Structural Measures

Structural outcomes are those which define the capacity or infrastructure in healthcare. For example, nurse staffing ratios (number of nurses per patient in a hospital) is one common structural measure. Adoption of health information technology (such as an electronic health record) is another common structural measure.

Process Measures

Structure impacts process. A **process** is a linked set of activities necessary to achieve a goal or produce a deliverable. Process describes how work is accomplished. In healthcare, this includes clinical activities (such as diagnosis and treatment) but also administrative processes (such as how payments are made). Process determines outcomes to a large degree. Outcomes include better health status, functioning, quality of life, patient satisfaction, and value.

Process measures are those which describe the quality, volume, and performance of a clinical or business process. For example, a process measure could include whether a patient was provided aspirin on admission or discharge (as in the case of patients with cardiovascular disease) or adherence rates to specific medications. Process of care measures reflect the quality of care provided to patients in an organization.

Outcome Measures

Better processes produce better results. To improve processes, organizations should adopt a formalized approach to mapping out processes and looking for ways to streamline and simplify them. Outcome measures reflect the output of a process. An output measure can be as straightforward as mortality rate (e.g., survival to hospital discharge, in-hospital mortality). Readmission rates and rates of surgical or hospital-acquired infections are also very common institutional measures of outcomes. Other outcomes are disease specific, such as case-mix adjusted length of stay for acute myocardial infarction.

Finally, there are composite quality measures. Composite implies that they are summary measures, either for an organization or for a specific disease condition (e.g., sepsis, stroke, heart failure, diabetes). Typically, composite measures are a small subset of the most significant metrics for a disease. The National Quality Forum (www.qualityforum. org) maintains an active list of all quality metrics endorsed by various organizations and associations. **Healthcare Effectiveness Data and Information Set (HEDIS)** is one standardized database of quality measures used to assess physicians and providers across the country and is used by insurance providers and health plans to report and benchmark quality. HEDIS provides specific operational definitions for metrics to ensure consistency of reported measures. The National Committee for Quality Assurance maintains the active list of HEDIS quality measures (www.ncqa.org).

There are many other measure sets in existence. Hospitals and provider groups are often confused by which types of measures to embrace. There are literally several hundred different measures in use by organizations, health plans, and insurers. This is further confounded by professional societies which endorse their own disease-specific measures, such as diabetes or cancer. The Centers for Medicare and Medicaid Services (CMS) is one of the largest payers in care, through the Medicare and Medicaid programs. CMS is trying to bring clarity to quality measures, by reimbursing patients for their achievement of quality. Programs such as the Merit-based Incentive Payment System (MIPS) are quality programs which reimburse providers for quality (instead of quantity) and is a move toward **value-based payment** models. Value-based payment is an approach used by payers to ensure that providers focus on quality and value and not just quantity.

Plan-Do-Check-Act

The most basic four-step methodologies for continuous improvement are known as plan-do-check-act (PDCA) or alternatively as the plan-do-study-act (PDSA). Both PDCA and PDSA refer to the same basic process and have a focus on continuously refining results over time and incorporating those learnings into the system. **PDCA** is a methodology for continuous improvement.

Plan: This refers to the development of the guidelines, framework, and goals to achieve specific targets. Appropriate measures should be identified that are high priority and in need of improvement. Quantitative expectations should be developed for these measures as well.

Do: This phase represents the execution or implementation of the plan, whether that is implementation of a revised process or adoption of a new application. This involves applying specific improvement methods to work toward desired targets for each measure. Data collection and analysis are also part of this phase.

Check: This can also be referred to as "study". In this phase, we will measure and evaluate the data collected earlier against the plans. Statistical process control and other tools are often used to assess behavior of processes and to explore variations and trends in outcomes.

Act: In this phase, refinement and adjustments to the process should continue. If the process has achieved desired effects in a test environment, then these will be put into the full system. Some organizations first deploy small pilots to test feasibility. A **pilot** is a small-scale project used to test results before widespread deployment. They are extremely useful to ensure that all kinks are worked out, in both technology and process.

Six Sigma

One useful tool for analyzing a process is a **flowchart**. A flowchart is a visual diagram depicting the sequential actions, steps, inputs, and decisions in a process. Since most processes require information or physical flows between departments or even organizations, they can be displayed with or without swim lanes. A swim lane is a depiction of the boundaries between processes and the cross-functionality between various parties in order to execute the business process. These can be either horizontally or vertically displayed. A sample process flowchart with a few of the key symbols is shown in Figure 13.2, presented with horizontal swim lanes.

Six Sigma is a quality improvement method focused on eliminating defects and reducing variability through statistical process control. It gained significant attention because of the work of industrial organizations such as Motorola and General Electric (Pyzdek and Keller, 2014). The primary advantage of this method is its focus on variance reduction or reduced variability. It is an approach to solving problems that requires users to focus on the primary measures and to improve their problem solving and decision-making to get there.

First thing you might ask is why is it called Six Sigma? A **sigma** is the mathematical term for standard deviation, annotated by the Greek symbol (σ). Standard deviation is defined as the square root of the variance. What we know about managing process behavior is that if we seek a reduction in variability, we want most measures to hover around the average (also called mean and typically represented by the Greek symbol ($\bar{x}$)). For example, if it takes on average 20 minutes to perform a catheterization in an interventional cardiac laboratory, we ideally would want all cases to take around 20 minutes, not wide swings in either direction. In the optimal sense, assuming that the patient's underlying condition was the same (which I realize is a difficult assumption to make), then we want the first and the last case to be relatively the same in terms of process behavior and outcomes. Processes that are "in control" do not have wide swings and variation, so that one time it is 2 hours and the next it is 20 minutes. Reducing variation and consistency are the goals.

Standard deviation is the primary statistical measures of variability or dispersion in data observations. In a normally distributed set of data, +/– one standard deviation from the mean will include 68.2% of all observations, and two standard deviations represent 95% of all observations. **Normal**

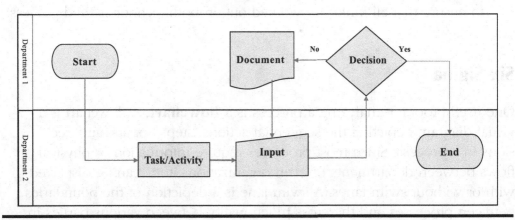

Figure 13.2 Process flowchart.

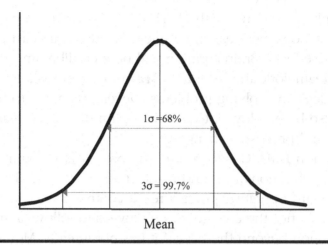

Mean

Figure 13.3   Normal distribution and sigma.

distributions of data have a larger denser concentration of observations toward the center and less on the sides (called tails). This assumes that we have enough observations of course. Statistically, we can ensure that data are normal when we calculate the mean, median, and the mode and they are identical or nearly identical. We also can calculate **skewness** (or asymmetry of the data) and **kurtosis** (heavily tailed in one direction or another) and ensure that both values are within normally defined ranges (usually +2 to −2) (Figure 13.3).

DMAIC

Six Sigma has a five-step cycle for improvement: DMAIC. **DMAIC** is an acronym for define, measure, analyze, improve, control. This is very similar in nature to the PDSA or PDCA process but focuses heavily on the upfront definition and measurement phase. It also places much more emphasis on statistical calculations and measurements. Define refers to understanding the problem and specifically defining what is wrong with it—is it not meeting customer requirements? Does it have excessive wait times? Are employees or stakeholders unhappy? Defining the problem is the first step toward improving it.

Measure is the quantification of the problem. It starts by exploring where current performance measures are and where they should be. Analyze requires a thorough understanding of the cause of the problem. Fishbone diagrams, Pareto analyses, process analysis, and other techniques will be required in this phase.

Improve is phase 4 of the method. This step is when the project team recommends solutions, verifies, and implements them, at least partially in a pilot, to observe effects. Brainstorming will be incredibly important, which requires good teamwork and listening. **Brainstorming** is a team approach to generating ideas and solving problems. Development of "to be" process maps should also be employed, to contrast again the "as is" maps, and show steps removed and processes changed.

The final step in DMAIC is to control the process and maintain a solution that can be operationalized and made stable over time. This requires changes to standard operating procedures, a control plan, and other documentation that codifies the change for employees to follow. It also should expand the solution beyond the pilot if it has not already. Monitoring and routinely re-evaluating the performance is essential to the control phase.

Six Sigma suggests that in normal data observations, we seek to minimize the number of sigma deviations away from the mean and to reduce the number of errors in the process. One way to do this is through measurement of actual failure rates, calculated as defects per million opportunities.

Managing Defects

Defects are errors in any clinical or operational process that creates harm, poor results, or variability in outcomes. The goal of performance improvement is to reduce errors, whether they are medical, medication, and other errors.

Defect per million opportunities (DPMO) is a calculation of defects observed on average divided by the number of opportunities for defects. The first is the idea of an outcome known as a "defect". A **defect** is any instance in a process where the customer requirement has not been met. In the example earlier involving nursing procedures, the outcome was positive (i.e., they were successfully completed in 17 minutes). If, however, it took 22 minutes for the procedures, and the patient was not able to have one of the three procedures completed, it would have been recorded as a defect, since it deviated from the expectation and did not meet the customer (or patient's) expectations. Another example would be an emergency department wait time. Assuming that a defective process would result in patients waiting more than 15 minutes (as an example), the frequency of visits greater than 15 minutes would be treated as process failures or defects.

Six Sigma uses a metric known as "Defect Per Million Opportunities" or DPMO to understand defect behavior for activities and processes. To calculate DPMO, analysts need to perform these four steps:

Step 1: Identify the process to evaluate the specific deliverables produced by the process. In our nursing example, the process is nursing procedures and the deliverables are successful completion of three procedures.

Step 2: Define successful outcomes and defects and count the total number of opportunities. In our example, we defined the defect earlier. The total opportunities would be defined as: (# of patients) × (# of procedures) × (frequency). For example, if we had 20 patients, each requiring three procedures twice a day, the total number of opportunities would be 120 (or 20 × 3 × 2).

Step 3: Obtain a statistical model of the process. In this step, the engineer should observe all the activities, gather the outcomes (as shown earlier), and statistically model the results, calculating the mean, standard deviation, and control limits. In addition, the total number of defects should be counted and recorded. For example, if the engineer observed all 120 opportunities in 1 day and counted eight defects (or instances that did not conform to requirements), then the DPMO would be calculated as: (8 ÷ 120) * 1,000,000 = 66,667. Therefore, in this example, the defects per million opportunities would be 66,667 (0.06667×10^6).

Step 4: Measure Sigma Level and Manage Improvements. After calculating the DPMO, it is compared to a Six Sigma Level in order to obtain a measure of improvement opportunities. Six Sigma actually refers to the calculation where only 3.4 defects per million is recorded, which yields a 99.99966% success rate. This yield can be calculated by subtracting from 100% the defect rate (e.g., 100% − (3.4/1,000,000) = 100 − 0.00034 = 0.99966, or 99.9%). Figure 13.4 allows you to graphically compare your process defect rates against sigma and DPMO levels. Using the example from earlier (with over 66,000 DPMOs), this would indicate Sigma level 3.

Process Capability Index

One other useful analytical tool that Six Sigma has provided us is process capability index (often expressed as C_p). A **process capability index** is a measure for gauging the extent to which a process meets the customer's expectations. Calculating it requires knowledge of the upper and lower control limits on the process behavior. It is mathematically defined as follows:

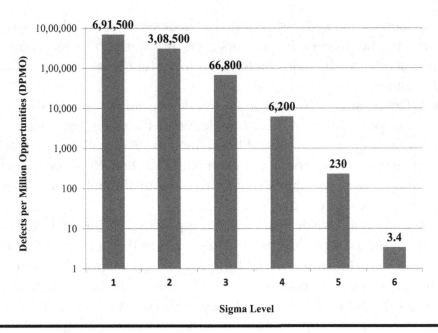

Figure 13.4   Six sigma levels and DPMO.

$$\left(\text{Upper Standard Limit} - \text{Lower Standard Limit}\right) \div 6\sigma$$

A $C_p > 1$ suggests that the process is capable, but it does not have any relation to the performance target, nor does it suggest that the process meets the customers' expectations. To improve on this, other complimentary metrics should be used (such as C_{pk}). C_{pk} is defined as the minimum of either of these formulas:

$$C_{pu}\left[(\text{USL} - \bar{x}) \div 3\sigma\right] \text{ or } C_{pl}\left[\bar{x} - \text{LSL}) \div 3\sigma\right]$$

Six Sigma Benefits

A few years ago, some colleagues and I performed a systematic review of the Six Sigma results published in peer-reviewed journals over a 15-year period (DelliFraine et al., 2013). What we found was quite interesting. We observed that most of the published accounts of outcomes did not consider changes in pre- versus post-performance of DPMO, process capability index, or any other statistical metric. Results were widely varied, and most did not use numerical values to report the magnitude of change. Although Six Sigma has a wide following, and can work, it needs to be conducted rigorously.

There will be benefits to focusing on process variation reduction, and these should be carefully observed and recorded and results should be shared with other organizations to help the industry improve.

Lean

Lean is a quality improvement method focused on removing waste and unnecessary steps from processes. The car manufacturer Toyota in Japan developed Lean. Lean quality management initiatives create standardized and stable processes to provide the best quality services or products as efficiently as possible. Any less than an ideal outcome is investigated immediately in order to identify the root cause and to resolve the problem. Lean philosophy embraces a continuous improvement strategy that supports creating simple and direct pathways and eliminating loops and duplication. Lean methods attempt to aggressively remove all "non-value-added" activities from a process. Non-value added means any step which does not produce value for the customer or is not essential to producing the final service. The primary approach is to standardize production and business processes so that flow can be leveled and all waste or inefficiencies removed.

Lean uses different tools and techniques to remove waste and improve quality. A key task is to delineate value-added activities from those which do not add value. Processes should seek to remove the non-value-added steps. Value is defined from the customer's perspective. The method for understanding this is through value streams. **Value stream mapping** is a technique where all tasks and actions in a process are modeled visually to show all activities performed from start to finish. Value stream mapping is used to identify those which add value versus those which do not. It is particularly useful to understand cross-functional tasks (i.e., across departments).

The key steps involve preparation for the mapping, data collection for current process, documentation of desired future state, and then execution of the map. A sample value stream map is shown below, using the visual symbols common for inventory, information flow, and waste as an example (Figure 13.5).

Lean has many other tools. **Kanban** is a visual card process (think post-it-notes on a whiteboard), which visually provides process flow and identifies bottlenecks. These cards work off the principle that the

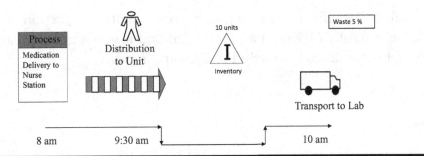

Figure 13.5   Value stream map.

brain can process visual information easier than reports or numerical data, so they are often used to trigger changes to process for continuous improvement.

Lean also uses a tool called **5S**. These are called that literally because they all start with the letter "s". Each step in this process helps to create the environment (working conditions) for optimizing value-added activities. The 5S are as follows:

- Sort
- Set in order
- Shine
- Standardize, and
- Sustain

Lean Versus Six Sigma

Six Sigma and Lean are often confused and sometimes combined into Lean Six Sigma. To compare their similarities and differences is important. Overarching goals are fairly similar between both methods, but Lean focuses on doing the right things (value-adding activities) and Six Sigma focuses on doing things right (with no errors). Lean also requires a more traditional methodology centered around Deming's PDSA (plan, do, study, act) cycle. Six Sigma relies on a similar approach called DMAIC. Lean utilizes leadership and training roles such as "sensei" (master teacher) and diffusion of beliefs and cultural value shifts much more than diffusion of analytical techniques. Table 13.1 compares the two methods.

Table 13.1   Six Sigma and Lean Comparison

Dimension	Six Sigma	Lean
Goals	Conformance to customer requirements; Elimination of defects (errors, re-work)	Remove non-value-added activities; Eliminate waste (errors, wait times)
Approach	Reduction of process variability	Standardization, production flow leveling
Principal Tool/ Method	Statistical process control, run charts, cause-and-effect diagrams	Value Stream Mapping, Kanban, 5S
Infrastructure	Through formalized structures, titles, and roles	Cultural change; "Sensei" relationships
Methodology	DMAIC (define, measure, analyze, improve, control)	PDSA (plan, do, study, act)
Performance Metrics	Quantifiable, cost of quality; mapped into financial value	Not consistent; Often result in new metrics

Source: Langabeer et al. (2009).

Theory of Constraints

Theory of constraints is a quality improvement method which addresses the effect of system constraints on performance outcomes (Goldratt and Cox, 1984). Theory of constraints (TOC) was conceptualized by Dr. Eliyahu Goldratt, a leading quality improvement researcher originally from Israel. TOC primarily has been used to address constraints. A **constraint** is a bottleneck or place where process throughput is limited. TOC focuses on identifying these places where constraints occur, and either fixing them or removing them entirely. In this focus on removing bottlenecks, it is similar to Lean's use of Kanban.

Goldratt contends that reducing obstacles that choke throughput will speed up (improve velocity of) processes, which will result in positive outcomes. There are definitely opportunities in healthcare to explore constraints—everything from wait lines in clinical departments and pharmacies to supply and inventory management concerns. Exploring where personnel shortages, system failures, or lack of products exist is necessary. Targeting the constraint and implementing these changes are key to certain types of improvements, although possibly less so on the clinical side and more on the administrative side. If a process seems to be impacted by issues of throughput, by optimizing supply (available capacity) or demand, then use of a TOC approach would be most suitable.

Process Modeling

Business and clinical processes involve complexities not only of the types of activities involved but also their timing and hand-offs between departments. **Process mapping** is a visual flowchart of ordered activities in a discrete process. It is also commonly called process flow. It starts by comprehensively defining all aspects of the process and placing them in flows on a chart. A sample flowchart was shown earlier in this chapter.

Converting these data into time period is best done with a run chart. A **run chart** is a line graph of key data plotted over time. Run charts should be used to graphically represent changes in outcomes or important variables over time, to analyze trends and patterns which might emerge. They are especially helpful to plot data to see if changes (a new project or process improvement) have worked, by comparing data over time. They can also help to easily identify if seasonality or other trends emerge. For example, a hospital could plot their data average length of stay (ALOS) metrics by time period (hourly, daily, weekly, monthly, annually). When you see data presented like this, it helps to easily spot highs and lows and direction of change. Generally speaking, the more granular or detailed the data, the more likely a pattern will emerge that is actionable. Figure 13.6 shows a run chart which plots ALOS by month.

Modeling is the conversion of the process into an analytical model to represent and simulate behaviors given changes in the key components. The process model therefore must detail, consequently each activity and responsible entity. The components for process modeling should attempt to define each of these:

- *Activity*: A task which occurs at a specific point in time, has a duration that is random, and shows a known probability distribution function.
- *Time*: Key parameter of a process, defined as the differential between the time an activity started and ended.
- *Resources*: Both inputs and outputs of a process should be defined.

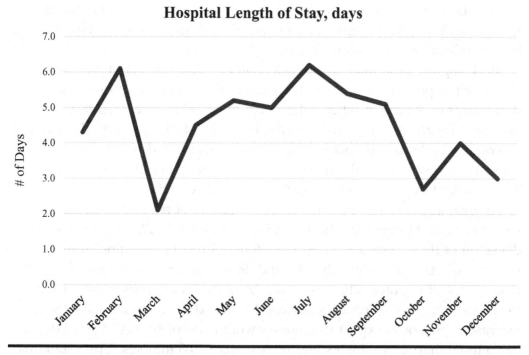

Figure 13.6   Process run chart

- *Event*: The culmination of an activity, which can change the state of a process.
- *Outcomes*: The results of the activities and events, most commonly expressed in a metric to gauge success and failure.

Most methodologies attempt to model each activity and event, by carefully observing and documenting these components defined above. For example, if a nurse entered a room to take vital signs at 10:05 am and left at 10:22 with three procedures completed, the output matrix would look like what is shown in Table 13.2.

After adequate observation of these activities, which normally involves a significant period of time, the process can be modeled using traditional process flowchart tools. More importantly, the *behavior* of the activities can be statistically analyzed. This is one of the main contributions of Six Sigma and

Table 13.2   Process Model

Activity	Time	Resources	Event	Outcome
Nurse intervention	17 minutes, 0 seconds	Nurse time, three units supply	Nurse completes three procedures	Successful

other data-driven methods. While some may argue that Six Sigma has no role in medicine, we disagree and believe that all processes can benefit from better understanding of their behaviors.

Modeling the time intervals allows engineers to understand the variability of the process. Since variability refers to the degree of dispersion of data points over time, it reflects the range of possible outcomes of a given process. The greater the variability, the less control that exists in the process outcomes. As discussed above, in a normally distributed set of data, +/– one standard deviation from the mean will include 68.2% of all observations. Two standard deviations represent 95% of all observations.

For example, assume we have 11 observations of nursing data, ranging from 11 to 23 minutes. The mean is approximately 17, and the standard deviation of these data are 3.193. Therefore, within 1σ deviation from the mean would be approximately 20.2 and 2σ (or the 95% confidence interval) would be 23.4 minutes. Therefore, in 68% of the cases, nurses were likely to complete their 3 procedures between 13.8 and 20.2 minutes. In 95% of the cases, you could expect that nurses would complete their 3 procedures in no more than 23.4 minutes and no less than 10.6 minutes. Understanding the behavior of data at a statistical level allows engineers to truly understand expectations and map out realistic process models. Figure 13.7 shows the concept of statistical process control graphically.

Software to enable simulation of process modeling is widely available. Tools (such as Simul8 and Arena Software) allow for discrete event simulations to be automated, to model key variables (resources, events) to simulate change in outcomes. **Discrete event simulation** is the dynamic modeling of discrete (separate) events to predict overall process and system behaviors. Discrete event simulation works on a graphical layer.

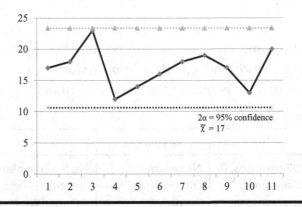

Figure 13.7   Statistical process control.

Similarly, Monte Carlo simulation uses mathematical calculations incorporating risk to predict decisions and outcomes. Monte Carlo simulation allows you to use spreadsheets or databases and is built into a number of software solutions (such as Palisade @RISK and Oracle Crystal Ball). Tools such as these allow for multiple iterations and estimations to give better predictions of potential changes in a process.

Other Tools and Techniques

Root Cause Analysis is an in-depth process or technique for identifying the fundamental factor beneath any variation in performance. **Root cause** is the primary, underlying reason behind an effect (or outcome). Root cause is the primary initiating cause. It is the most basic factor of a specific effect. Root cause analysis should focus quality teams on identifying the underlying mechanisms for poor performance or variation in a process. The emphasis should be on the *process* and *management systems,* not on departments or individuals.

Cause-and-effect analysis is a technique to identify the feasible causes that are related to a specific problem. Typically, cause-and-effect diagrams identify all causes of an effect and then narrow down the analysis to the primary, underlying causes. Cause-and-effect diagrams (also called **fishbone** or Ishikawa) display visually the results of the analysis to make it easier for others to conceptualize and act on (Figure 13.8).

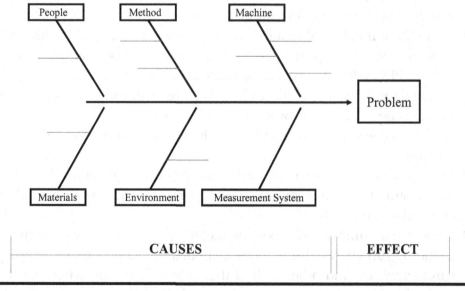

Figure 13.8   Cause-and-effect diagram (fishbone).

Function	Failure Mode	Effect	Cause	Controls	Action Taken	Owner
Minimize patient wait times	No rooms available	Patient boarded outside room	Lack of rooms	System generated alerts	ED Chief to convert private rooms	Jim L
		Patient wait times excessive	Lack of nursing personnel	Nurse manager manages wait times	Additional personnel recruitment	
		Patient leaves without being seen				

Figure 13.9 Failure effects and modes analysis.

Failure modes and effects analysis (FMEA) is a tool for documenting potential failures in a process, causes, risks, and potential solutions. FMEA is primarily used to document failures in a process, and clearly specify causes, controls, and actions to mitigate such failures in the future. FMEA is particularly useful when the majority of the poor outcomes (results) are due to a limited number of modes (Figure 13.9).

Chapter Summary

- The Donabedian model helps to provide an underlying framework for explaining how inputs are converted into outputs in healthcare. Structure and process determine outcomes.
- There are a number of quality methodologies available for health systems to follow to improve performance. The most popular of these include PDCA/PDSA, Six Sigma, Lean, and Theory of Constraints.
- Six Sigma is a great analytical tool which uses statistical process control to bring the behavior of processes under control.
- Lean helps organizations focus on reducing waste and non-value-added activities.
- Theory of constraints works well when you see signs of bottlenecks (or constraints on capacity) that limit your organization to respond to demand responsively.
- There are a number of process management tools to choose from, including run charts, discrete event simulation, value stream mapping, Pareto analysis, and others. All of them should be used where most applicable in a process improvement project.

Discussion Questions

1. What does DMAIC stand for? How have you seen it in use at your organization?
2. What is the difference between a process of care, structure, and outcome quality measure?
3. Why is the concept of sigma and deviations so important to process control?
4. How does the type of issue your organization faces impact the choice of performance improvement methodology?
5. How is value stream mapping different from process flowcharting?

Key Terms

5S; Brainstorming; Cause-and-Effect Analysis; Constraint; Defect; Defect per Million Opportunities (DPMO); Discrete Event Simulation; DMAIC; Donabedian Model; Failure Modes and Effect Analysis; Fishbone Diagram; HEDIS; Kanban; Kurtosis; Lean; Modeling; Normal Distribution; PDCA; Pilot; Process; Process Capability Index; Process Mapping; Root Cause; Root Cause Analysis; Run Chart; Sigma; Six Sigma; Skewness; Standard Deviation; Theory of Constraints; Value Stream Mapping; Value-Based Payment; Variability

References

DelliFraine J, Wang M, McCaughey D, Langabeer J, and Erwin C (2013). The use of six sigma in healthcare management: are we using it to its full potential? *Quality Management in Health Care, 22*(3), 210–223.

Donabedian A (2005). Evaluating the quality of medical care. *Milbank Quarterly, 83*(4), 691–729.

Goldratt E and Cox J (1984). *The Goal.* New York: Routledge Publishing.

Langabeer J, DelliFraine J, Heineke J, and Abbass I (2009). Implementation of lean and six sigma quality initiatives in hospitals: a goal theoretic perspective. *Operations Management Research, 2*(1), 13–27.

National Committee for Quality Assurance (2017). Healthcare Effectiveness Data and Information Set (HEDIS) Measures. Available at www.ncqa.org

National Quality Forum (2017). Available at www.qualityforum.org

Pyzdek T and Keller P (2014). *The Six Sigma Handbook* (4th ed). New York: McGraw-Hill Education.

Chapter 14

The Practice of Strategy

Bringing It All Together

As described throughout this book, there are several different factors impacting the performance and strategy for healthcare organizations. Certainly, the industry will see changes tomorrow that we have not even imagined. Today, the industry is grappling with how to improve medical technology to get closer to patients, through artificial intelligence and digital transformation that will help organizations be more consumer centric. Population health management, telehealth, and remote patient monitoring are also becoming more advanced, as healthcare delivery moves outside of hospital walls. Interoperability will also become more important, with the ability to seamlessly share data between apps, providers, and multiple partners within the healthcare value chain. Re-examining how health is reimbursed, through value-based payments and bundled care, will force a higher focus on cost-effectiveness. Rapid deployment of new vaccines to deal with future pandemics also need to be part of the agenda. Public health in general will undergo significant transformations going forward as well.

Bottom Line: change, innovation, and a heightened focus on value-based care, is coming to healthcare. Hospitals, clinics, pharmacies, and other organizations will have to address their core competencies and find a unique competitive advantage to continue to survive and thrive. The way to deal with this is through better real-time strategy adaptations, and performance management.

Leaders should also think about the 4 T's: trust, training, transparency, and teamwork. Trust-building with both your partners in the value chain,

DOI: 10.4324/9781032623726-17

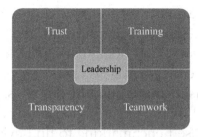

Figure 14.1   Here: leadership in healthcare organizations.

stakeholders, employees, and customers is essential to developing strong management systems. Employee's don't typically blindly follow managers because of their position, but rather they follow them because they are inspired by a culture of trust. Build a trusting relationship within the organization and it's stakeholders and value chain. Continuous learning and growth through training and development will be important for you and your team. Skillsets and cultural competencies change, invest in continuous training. Developing transparency in the decision-making and planning processes is expected from leaders today. Finally, cross-functional teamwork and collaboration between all departments is built only when employees see good teamwork at the top. Make teamwork a priority. Focus on these four areas to build your leadership and strategy arsenal (Figure 14.1).

Becoming a More Effective Healthcare Executive

Based on the trends, changes, and challenges we have discussed in this book, there is a simple question you should ask at this point: "how do I as a manager or executive become a more effective leader, capable of coping with strategic changes and continuous performance management?" Here are ten final tips to consider.

1. Develop a digital mindset and data-driven culture. A **digital mindset** can be defined as "a set of attitudes and behaviors that enable people and organizations to see how data, algorithms, and AI open up new possibilities" (Neeley and Leonardi, 2022). Chief Digital Officers (CDO) is now a new and common title in healthcare, as organizations figure out their approach to become consumer and patient-centric with their technologies. Stay ahead of the curve and develop a digital mindset.

2. Build an organizational culture that values question-asking and continuous improvement. The best way to do this is to simply ask the

question "why" repeatedly. Why are we doing things this way? Why is that the right way? Encourage your staff and colleagues to do the same. Asking questions, and being curious by nature, is one of the traits of successful leaders.

3. Adopt **evidence-based management** practices. Some processes need re-inventing or need fixing. Organizations don't always have to re-create the wheel though. Use benchmarking to find evidence-based practices that work and adapt those to your setting. Good management practices should become the norm, as we expect in our evidence-based clinical practice.

4. Learn to actively listen. Most people, and many executives, tend to speak more than they listen. This is not a good practice. Create a safe space for your employees to speak up. Show interest in what others have to say, and that encourages people to speak up and contribute. If you are one-on-one, give your undivided attention to those people. All of these active listening skills are vital as you move toward the top of the organization.

5. Recruit and retain the highest caliber staff you can afford. If you are a manager of two people, don't be afraid to hire people that are smarter than you! If you are an executive over hundreds, you had better have dozens of people smarter than you. Use your resources wisely to recruit and retain the best staff, physicians, and managers available. High caliber employees create much more value than they cost the organization.

6. Keep learning and growing. Learning organizations require all of us to constantly be on the top of our game. Learn about new and evolving techniques and analyses. Take courses in project management. Keep working on developing better interpersonal skills for teamwork and collaboration. Learn budgeting and accounting, and how your organization reports their financials. Try to learn one new thing every week, and by the end of each year, you will have amassed a library of new knowledge.

7. Built your leadership capacity. Chapters 6 and 7 focused on leadership qualities and characteristics. More than likely, you are strong in some and weak in others. Also continue to learn and explore leadership literacy by reading quality magazines, listening to speakers, and attending conferences. Here's some strategies to keep improving.

   a. Use a 360° tool to receive your teammates, colleagues, and direct reports feedback about yourself. Even if your human resources department doesn't require it, ask anyway for input on a voluntary basis. Measuring your leadership performance should be utilized where possible, using that feedback to keep growing and improving (Conger, 2004).

b. Also consider the use of a leadership coach—somebody that can help perform an assessment on you, and whom you can rely on for tips on how to handle specific situations. Try to develop in areas that you find gaps.

8. Leadership involves putting other people first and developing others' potential by using facilitation and interpersonal skills to keep people engaged and participating. Learning to identify what motivates others and encourage teamwork are critical skills. Leadership will help analysts and project managers continue to move up the organizational hierarchy.

9. Be a strategic thinker and keep asking questions. As we've discussed in this book, strategic thinking skills help to keep you in front of the competition, refining and adapting plans as needed. Don't let your strategy processes become stale. Keep asking tough questions and use all intelligence signals to focus on your competitive advantage.

10. Stay optimistic and build an organizational culture that is positive and hopeful for the future. Yes, you need to build a great strategy and vision and work hard to make those plans come to fruition with good management systems. But don't forget a positive outlook. This helps employees get excited about their roles and be more engaged in the organization.

11. Keep up the hard work. The hardest part about any undertaking is to stick with it over the long term. Keep going, and keep striving for greatness.

Chapter Summary

■ New changes and trends will impact healthcare strategy in the future. Be sure to stay on top of these and monitor their impact on your organization.

■ Follow the ten tips for becoming a better leader.

Discussion Questions

1. What additional set of challenges does your organization face beyond those mentioned here? How are you tackling those?
2. How are you preparing to increase your skills and competencies in leadership? What is working and what is not?
3. How would you rate your current CEO in terms of their leadership capabilities? What areas are lacking, and how do you know if you yourself have these covered?

Key Terms

Digital Mindset
Evidence-based Management

References

Conger JA (2004). Developing leadership capability: what's inside the black box. *Academy of Management Executive, 18*(3), 136–139.

Neeley T and Leonardi P (2022). Developing a digital mindset. *Harvard Business Review*, May-June 2022, p. 50–55.

Glossary of Key Terms

5S Concept used in Lean to reduce waste. Sort, set in order, shine, standardize, and sustain.

Acquisition Type of growth strategy in which one organization acquires another organization.

Alignment Harmony and synchronization between decisions and plans. Consistency between strategy and supporting processes and practices.

Balanced scorecard A set of measures that give top managers a fast and comprehensive view of the organization's performance.

Behavioral congruence Alignment of our analytical reasoning with our intuitive and emotional processing.

Benchmarking The comparison of a key performance measurement relative to the competition or other leading organizations.

Board effectiveness assessment A formal evaluation of the board's contributions and overall effectiveness, sometimes referred to as board audit.

Board of directors The highest level of governance for an organization.

Board structure The board's composition, rules, and procedures.

Bounded rationality Concept that we as humans possess only a limited, finite capacity to understand all options available to us.

Brainstorming A team approach to generating novel ideas and solving problems.

Business case The justification behind a project, but in many cases, the measures of improvement are very qualitative and intangible.

Cause-and-effect analysis Technique to identify feasible causes related to a specific problem. Also called fishbone diagram.

Change A transition from one state to another.

Change management Activities involved in helping people adapt to changes in an organization.

Charter (board) The mission or purpose that the board officially holds beyond the fiduciary basics and hiring and firing the CEO.

Communications (board) Transfer of information in both directions between the board and the management team.

Competition When two or more players in a market attempt to reach or serve the same group of customers, with both trying to gain an advantage over the other to win a share of the market. Existence of substitute providers of a product or service.

Competitive advantage A condition that causes you to be in a favorable position relative to your competitors.

Competitive intelligence The process of gathering, analyzing, interpreting, and disseminating specific information about competing healthcare providers' processes and practices. Information about your competitors and markets.

Competitive strategy Strategy and choices that are focused on how to win over your competition.

Competitiveness The ability of an organization to provide goods and services that are superior to rivals and produces value for customers and long-term sustainability.

Composition (board) The structure and functioning of the board.

Consistency (board) Uniformity of the information and governance process.

Constraint A bottleneck or place where process throughput is limited.

Contribution (board) Effectiveness that boards bring by actively contributing, being engaged, and adding value.

Control (board) A central board or governance process involving setting of direction for an organization.

Cost of quality The sum of all costs associated with providing inferior, error-prone, or poor-quality services.

Data-driven management The application of proven and established organizational practices to improve decisions and results.

Democratic leadership A leadership style which helps to lead to innovative solutions and high levels of employee buy-in.

Decision The output of a process and selection among multiple alternatives.

Decision quality Refers to how good the process was when making a decision, irrespective of the actual outcome.

Decision rights These identify the types of decisions that can be made to align with strategy, who can make those decisions, what spending limit they are authorized for, and who will be involved in making them.

Defect Any instance in a process where the customer requirement has not been met.

DPMO Defect per million opportunities is a calculation of defects observed on average divided by the number of opportunities for defects.

Digital mindset A set of attitudes and behaviors that enable people and organizations to see how data, algorithms, and AI open up new possibilities.

Directors A member of the board of directors, a key part of organizational governance.

Discovery A thorough investigation of the present environment and collection of evidence.

Discrete event simulation Dynamic modeling of discrete (separate) events to predict overall process and system behaviors.

DMAIC An acronym for Define, Measure, Analyze, Improve, Control. A type of process improvement.

Donabedian model A structural framework for examining quality of care.

Electronic health record A comprehensive longitudinal electronic record that stores patient health data in a hospital or clinic.

Entrepreneur Somebody that starts something new, such as a new business or company.

Evidence Empirical data, or proof, supporting a decision or position.

Evidence-based management The use of best practices and strategic thinking to identify the best evidence to apply within an organization.

Execution Actions involved in putting your decisions and plans into effect. Also known as implementation.

Flawless execution We mean implementing plans nearly perfectly without a major glitch or error.

Fiduciary Responsibilities involving trust, and doing what is in the best financial interest of the organization.

Failure Modes and Effects Analysis (FMEA) A tool for documenting potential failures in a process, causes, risks, and potential solutions.

Fishbone Also called Ishikawa or cause-and-effect diagrams; it displays visually the results of the analysis to make it easier for others to conceptualize.

Goals Broad, long-term statements of an ideal future state.

Flowchart A visual diagram depicting the sequential actions, steps, inputs, and decisions in a process.

Governance The activities, decision processes, and systems used to effectively provide oversight and financial accountability for the organization.

Habit A behavior that is so ingrained that it requires almost no conscious thought.

HEDIS Healthcare Effectiveness Data and Information Set (HEDIS). One standardized database of quality measures used to assess physicians and providers across the country and is used by insurance providers and health plans to report and benchmark quality.

Heuristics Mental shortcuts that reduce the burden on our mind.

Hunches The use of intuition or gut-level instincts in decision-making.

Implementation Actions involved in putting your decisions and plans into effect. Also known as execution.

Improvement Positive change or transition from something in a steady state to something better.

Informationalization Data are integrated into a product.

Intrapreneur Somebody that starts a new business or department within an existing company.

Inputs Information or data points that are used in processing to assess how one should make a decision.

Insolvency An organization's inability to pay its debt and obligations.

Kaizen The Japanese word for continuous improvement.

Kanban A visual card process (think post-it-notes on a whiteboard), which visually provides process flow and identifies bottlenecks.

Key performance indicators (KPI) Quantitative measures of performance used to evaluate the success that an organization has in meeting established objectives.

Kurtosis Data that are heavily tailed in one direction, used in statistical process control.

Leadership style The leader's system of providing overarching direction, planning, deciding, and motivating employees within an organization.

Lean A quality improvement method focused on removing waste and unnecessary steps from processes.

Management engineering The application of engineering principles to healthcare processes.

Management systems Processes, practices, procedures, and information systems that help to keep organizations in alignment, balanced, and in control.

Market segments Targeting of specific customers by market.

Mergers A combination of any portion of two organizations' assets and operations regardless of the financial or legal structure the deal takes. Characterized by combining people, departments, systems, processes, locations, products, and services from at least two disparate organizations to one common organization.

Mergers and acquisitions A form of growth strategy involved by joining or acquiring another organization.

Minutes (board) Board minutes are official written record of a board meeting.

Modeling The conversion of the process into an analytical model to represent and simulate behaviors given changes in the key components.

Morbidity A measure of the rate of illness within a population.

Mortality A measure of the rate of incidence for deaths within a population.

Normal distributions Describes data that have a larger denser concentration of observations toward the center and less on the sides (called tails).

Objectives Specific, short-term, quantifiable statements that are readily measurable.

Operational excellence A uniform practice of delivering on goals, also referred to as flawless execution.

Optimism A generalized belief that future outcomes will usually be positive.

Organic growth A form of organizational growth which occurs when you get a new customer for existing facilities, using existing resources.

Organizational culture The collective beliefs, values, assumptions, structure, systems, stories, and even biases that are shared by all members of the company or organization.

Pareto Chart A combination bar/line graph depicting individual and cumulative frequency represented in descending order.

PDCA Plan, do, check, act. PDCA is a methodology for continuous improvement.

Performance The result, capabilities, or outcomes of a process or organization.

Performance improvement An approach that analyzes, measures, and changes business and clinical processes to improve outcomes.

Performance management The process by which organizations implement their strategies, and align their resources, systems, and employees to strategic objectives.

Pilot Small-scale project used to test results before widespread deployment.

Process A linked set of activities necessary to achieve a goal or produce a deliverable.

Process capability index A measure for gauging the extent to which a process meets the customer's expectations.

Process mapping A visual flowchart of ordered activities in a discrete process.

Project An organized effort involving a sequence of activities that are temporarily being performed to achieve a desired outcome.

Project management The application of knowledge, skills, tools, and techniques to project activities to meet the project requirements.

Quality The perception of the level of value a customer places on an organization's outputs, and the degree to which these meet established specifications and benchmarks.

Quality management A management philosophy focused on systematically improving performance and processes.

Rightsizing Developing optimal staffing levels within a product line.

Risks Describe potential exposures that may cause harm, also known as threats.

Root cause The primary underlying reason behind an effect.

Root cause analysis In-depth technique to identify the fundamental factors beneath variation in outcomes.

Run chart A way to visualize performance or behavior using a line graph of key data plotted over time.

Servant leadership A leadership style that emphasizes increasing service to others, a holistic approach to work, and promoting a sense of community.

Service line A discrete group of closely related product items, such as the number of medical offerings available in the portfolio.

Sigma The mathematical term for standard deviation, annotated by the Greek symbol (σ).

Six Sigma A quality improvement method focused on eliminating defects and reducing variability through statistical process control.

Skewness Asymmetry of the data, used for statistical process control.

Standard deviation The primary statistical measures of variability or dispersion in data observations.

Statistical process control (SPC) The term used for applying statistics to monitor and control the behavior of a process.

Stochastic Something, such as a decision, that is based on chance and probabilities as opposed to deterministic.

Storytelling The ability for leaders to connect people and inspire them to take action.

Strategic alliances Partnerships between multiple organizations to help support organizational growth strategy.

Strategic decision-making Decision processes that occur at the highest levels of an organization and typically involves major commitments of resources or changes in strategic direction.

Strategic fit Alignment of leadership style with the individual's personality and characteristics, and alignment of the strategy to the environment.

Strategic intelligence A collection of key information about your competitors, market, risks, and products that help enable long-term organizational success.

Strategic planning The process by which strategies are developed or formulated and alternative directions are conceived.

Strategic positioning Aligning your intended strategy with all of these external and internal factors to ensure success.

Strategy The pattern of high-impact choices that determine the strategic direction for an organization.

Structural alignment Focuses on the alignment, or coordination and collaboration, between the overarching organizational strategy to each functional unit. Also refers to alignment between the organizational vision and its strategic and operational decisions.

SWOT (strengths, weaknesses, opportunities, and threats) A type of analysis used to understand your organization and the industry overall.

Systems orientation Interconnected activities and processes where change in one area produces change elsewhere.

Theory of constraints A quality improvement method which addresses the effect of system constraints on performance outcomes.

Transactional leadership A leadership style characterized by setting clear expectations and providing rewards for performance.

Transition plan The set of steps and activities necessary to prepare for the full integration following a merger or acquisition.

Transformational leadership A leadership style that inspires and motivates their teams to achieve higher levels of performance and innovation.

Trade-offs Compromises between two or more choices.

Value The relationship between outcomes produced by an organization and costs over time.

Value-based payment An approach used by payers to ensure that providers focus on quality and value and not just quantity.

Value stream mapping A technique where all tasks and actions in a process are modeled visually to show all activities performed from start to finish.

Variability The relative degree of dispersion of data points, especially as they differ from the norm.

Zero defect A philosophy that expects managers to prevent errors before they begin, which reduces total costs by doing things right the first time.

Appendix 1: Checklist of Strategic Planning Questions

External Analysis

Customer Analysis

- What motivates customers to buy patient care or to seek care at a specific hospital?
- What attributes of the care are important?
- What value-added services, in addition to the actual delivery of care, are desirable?
- What objectives do customers seek?
- What changes in motivation are occurring or could occur?
- Are customers satisfied?
- Are there any unmet needs?

Competitor Analysis

- Who are all competitors we face in our markets?
- How many competitors are there? How concentrated is the market?
- How strong a foothold do they have on the market?
- Why are competitors able to sustain market share?
- Which competitors should we focus our attentions on? What are their strengths?
- What plans do our competitors have for the short and long terms?
- What does our competitors systems and networks look like? How effective are they?

- How fast are our competitors growth rates? In what products?
- How profitable are our key competitors?
- What are our competitor's strengths and weaknesses?

Industry Analysis

- What trends are occurring today that is changing healthcare dynamics?
- What healthcare financing issues do we need to worry about for academic medicine?
- What are the industry's key success factors?

Environmental Analysis

- What new healthcare technologies are being explored?
- What technologies are considered breakthrough that might revolutionize the industry?
- What will be their impact on our organization, and our ability to deliver service in those areas?
- What competitors are leading the advancement of these technologies?
- Have any of our competitors progressed further in adopting or implementing these technologies?
- How and when will mobile apps, artificial intelligence, telemedicine, and remote monitoring impact our organization?
- How will electronic commerce and Blockchain be used for healthcare transactions? Are we prepared?
- What opportunities and threats exist?
- What scenarios can we imagine that might cause us to re-think our strategies?
- What are emerging lifestyle trends?
- What changes are occurring in the population?
- What will be the implications of these changes on healthcare and our organization?
- What opportunities might exist for new programs?
- How is family per capital income changing in our market?
- What trends are occurring in unemployment rates?
- What effects might the stock market or inflation rates have on healthcare consumption?
- Will regulatory or legislative reforms, such as the Balanced Budget Amendment, impact our organization? How?

Internal Analysis

Strategy Analysis

- Is our current strategy effective?
- Are we being responsive to the needs of changing customer demographics?
- What issues exist that are not covered in our strategy?
- Do weaknesses exist that competing hospitals are exploiting?

Performance Analysis

- How does our current performance compare to other hospitals?
- What are our core competencies? What are our distinctive competencies?
- Is our current service line portfolio sufficient?

Financial Analysis

- Where should we be re-investing resources?
- How does our cost structure compare to other hospitals? To other teaching hospitals?
- Are our financial resources adequate to achieve our goals?

Structure, Style, and Systems

- Does our organizational structure allow us to achieve desired results?
- Is our management style appropriate for our current condition?
- Are their gaps in our senior leadership skillsets?
- What internal issues exist that are preventing us from successful strategy execution?

Index

Note: **Bold** page numbers refer to tables and *italic* page numbers refer to figures.

Printed in the United States
by Baker & Taylor Publisher Services